FRANCE

160 km/100 miles

NORTH SEA

North Channel

Dundee
Glasgow
Firth of Forth
Edinburgh

Randers
Arhus
DENMARK

Esbjerg
Odense
Fyn

Belfast

ISLE OF MAN

Irish Sea

Newcastle
Sunderland
Carlisle
Middlesbrough
UNITED

Flensburg
North Frisian Islands
Lolland
Kiel
Lübeck

York
Leeds
Kingston upon Hill
Manchester
Liverpool
Sheffield
Stoke
Nottingham
Derby
Leicester
Wolverhampton
Birmingham
Coventry
Norwich
Cambridge
Ipswich
KINGDOM

Frisian
Islands
Groningen
NETHER LANDS
Amsterdam
Bremen
Hamburg
Hannover
ELBE
Münster
Bielefeld
Dortmund
Essen
Kassel
Düsseldorf
Wuppertal
FED. REP. OF GERMANY
Köln
Erfu

Wales
Swansea
Cardiff
BRISTOL CHANNEL
Bristol
Oxford
Reading
LONDON
Southampton
Portsmouth
Bournemouth
Brighton
Dover
Calais
Oostende
ISLE OF WIGHT
Plymouth

Jsselmeer
The Hague
Utrecht
Rotterdam
Antwerpen
Bruxelles
BELGIUM
Lille
Liège
Bonn
Koblenz
Wiesbaden
Frankfurt
RHEIN
Mannheim

English Channel

GUERNSEY
JERSEY
Cherbourg
Le Havre
Rouen
Saint Quentin
Reims
LUX.
Luxemburg
Metz
Saarbrücken
Karlsruhe
Stuttgart

CÔTES D'ARMOR
Saint Malo
Brest
FINISTÈRE
Lorient
MORBIHAN
ILLE ET VILAINE
Rennes
SEINE
Paris
Versailles
Nancy
Strasbourg
Meuse
Troyes
Mulhouse
Donau

BELLE ILE
Nantes
Angers
Le Mans
Orléans
Tours
LOIRE
FRANCE
Dijon
Basel
Zürich
Bodensee

ATLANTIC
ILE DE RÉ
La Rochelle
Châteauroux
Allier
Besançon
Bern
SWITZERLAND
Lausanne
Geneva
Lake Geneva
ALPES

OCEAN
ILE D'OLÉRON
Limoges
Clermont-Ferrand
LOIRE
Lyon
Mont Blanc
4807m
Como
Bergar

Bordeaux
Brive
Dordogne
Saint Étienne
RHÔNE
Valence
Grenoble
Torino
Milano

Bay of Biscay
Garonne
Avignon
Nimes
Genova
ITAL
La Spezia

Santander
Bayonne
Pau
Toulouse
Montpellier
Béziers
Nice
MONACO
Ligurian Sea
CAP CORSE

Bilbao
San Sebastian
Pamplona
Pico de Aneto
3404m
PYRENEES
Perpignon
Marseille
Toulon
Cannes
Bastia

Burgos
Vitoria
Logroño
EBRO
Gerona
CORSE
Ajaccio

Valladolid
Duero
Zaragosa
MEDITERRANEAN SEA
SARDINIA
Sassari

SPAIN
Barcelona
Tarragona
Olbia

Bienvenue!

In the year 1887, the French poet Stephen Liègard entitled his book about France's Mediterranean coast *La Côte d'Azur*; thus one of the most impressive areas of France gained its name. This azure-blue coast is associated with summer, sun and vacations, with fashionable Cannes, Monte Carlo and St Tropez; with high society, glamour and the stuff of which dreams are made.

Imagine you have a friend on the Côte d'Azur, someone who knows the region like a native, someone willing to take you on an insider's tour of this exciting region. *Insight Pocket Guide: Côte d'Azur* is designed to familiarise you with this legendary stretch of coast, providing carefully worked out and personally formulated routes and tours.

Michaela Lentz, author of books for children and teenagers, of cookery books and novels, has lived in the area of Vence for 13 years. She has divided the Côte d'Azur and its attractive hinterlands into 22 regional sections. Her guide leads you from Nice through St Paul de Vence; from Cannes to St Tropez. You can follow her routes in sequence or pick out sections for a briefer tour.

Michaela begins with a brief historical outline which follows the development of the Côte d'Azur from pre-Christian times to the present day. Next you start out on your travels: in Nice you stroll down the Promenade des Anglais, eat ice cream at the renowned Hôtel Negresco, find out where the best onion cakes are to be had and get to know the old city and the distinguished Cimiez quarter. You continue via Villefranche to Monaco—the 'Eldorado' of the beautiful (and *rich*). In the process, Michaela shows you where local people prefer to spend their time.

Further stops along the way include the artists' town of St Paul de Vence, Vallauris—where Picasso once lived—the film city of Cannes, the uniquely beautiful Corniche d'Or, the appealing Maure Massif and St Tropez. Notes on where to dine well (and authentically), a chapter on Provençal cuisine and information about festivals and events as well as useful travel tips round out this fact-filled *Insight Pocket Guide: Côte d'Azur.*

Bienvenue! Welcome!

Insight Pocket Guide
Côte d'azur
Second English Edition

© **1992 APA Publications (HK) Ltd**

All Rights Reserved

Printed in Singapore by:
Höfer Press (Pte) Ltd, Singapore
Fax: 65-861 6438

INSIGHT *POCKET* GUIDES

CÔTE D'AZUR

Written by	**Michaela Lentz**
Directed by	**Hans Höfer**
Desidn Concept by	**V. Barl**
Art Direction by	**Willi Friedrich**
Photography by	**Oliver Lentz**
Editorial Director	**Chris Catling**

CARTE D'ACCÈS A BORD
BOARDING PASS

INSIGHT
pocket
GUIDES

C o n t e n t s

Dear Reader!

It must have been in 1951 that I came here for the first time. We visited Picasso, who was occupied with his work *War and Peace* in Vallauris. I fell in love with Picasso and his painting in that tiny Provençal village; I also fell in love with the people with their rustic, deeply tanned faces; with their eyes sparkling with the joy of life, with their gestures and laughter; with the warm January sun and with that particular light which attracts so many painters . . . of which I, however, knew absolutely nothing. This was a childish and rather mute love, to be sure, but it worked its way deeply into my soul. I carried it around with me and promised, secretly to myself, that I would yield to it one day.

It was a long time before I fulfilled this promise. On numerous return visits I re-examined my memories over and over again to see if my love had changed. Naturally, I noticed the disfigurements, the uncontrolled development, the apartment buildings—sins of concrete and steel—the gigantic supermarket and gas station complexes, the concessions made to mass tourism. The beloved, simple face of the place was undergoing change to be sure. Like the rest of the sun-filled Mediterranean, it was being loved too well by too many not to change.

But then my eyes came to rest on the gentle hills and the imposing Maritime Alps in the background; on the old villages in which narrow houses push up against each other like sheep seeking protection from the wind; on the loosely laid bricks in shades of tender ochre, rose and grey; on the orange, lemon and olive groves; and I observed the easy composure of the people, eaves-dropped on their animated conversations, admired the skill and

ease with which they manipulate their language, explored the solitude of the mountains and joined in the crowds on the coast. Then I fell in love again. Differently this time—more realistically perhaps, but more intensely as well.

Thirteen years ago I finally pitched my tent here for good. I live in an old farmhouse, only 10 minutes walk away from the centre of Vence, which, after painstaking restoration, has become a comfortable country home with a swimming pool, a *boule* court and a splendid shady terrace. In my love affair with Provence and the Côte d'Azur nothing has changed—in fact the reverse is true. That is why I am so glad to share it with all who visit me.

Mischa leutt

HISTORY

Sun and Sand, Ship and Shore

In the Grotto of Vallonet, archaeologists have found tools estimated to be 900,000 years old—the oldest in France. You can see evidence of how people lived here some 400,000 years ago in the archaeological finds on display at the Musée Terra Amata in Nice. The first historical milestones extend back to around 1000BC, when the Ligurians settled a broad stretch of the Mediterranean coast. In 600BC the Phocaean Greeks founded what is now Marseilles. They brought olive, fig, nut and cherry trees and grape vines—and they introduced the use of money.

In the 5th and 4th centuries BC the Greek settlers established trading posts in Hyères, St Tropez, Antibes, Nice and Monaco. Celts invaded southern France and intermarried with the Ligurians. In 122BC the Celts were defeated by the Romans. Under General Marius, the Romans went on to defeat the Teutons near Aix-en-Provence (Aquae Sextiae) in 102BC. In 49BC Caesar founded Fréjus (Forum Julii). In 6BC the 45 Alpine tribes finally submitted to Roman rule. To commemorate their victory over these tribes, the Romans built a 130ft (40m) tall victory monument at the feet of Mont Agel, where the Via Julia Augusta was built in the course of the battles. This superb example of Roman art, the Alpine Trophy, still stands to this day, at La Turbie overlooking Monaco. The Via Aurelia—which followed much the same course as the present-day *autoroute*—was one of the most important roads of the Roman Empire. It connected Rome with Arles by way of Genoa, Cimiez,

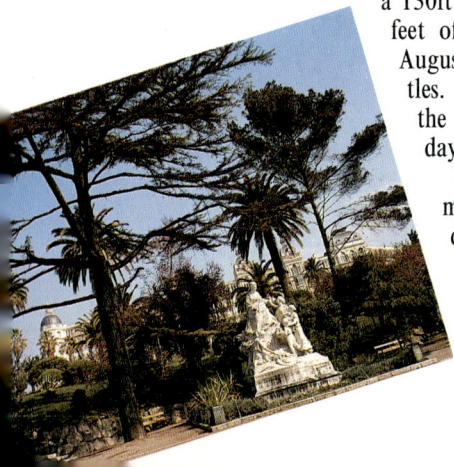

Culture

Antibes, Fréjus and Aix. Every 4850ft (1478m) there were marker stones indicating the distances (one such stone can be seen in the museum in St Raphael). Cimiez was then the administrative capital of the *Alpes Maritimae*. Excavations there convey an idea of the highly developed culture that the Romans brought with them.

The uncontested rule of the Romans brought the region a period of peace which lasted four centuries—the *Pax Romana*. In the 4th and 5th centuries the Vandals, Visigoths, Burgundians, Ostragoths and Franks all settled in southern France for a period. In 855, Provence was declared a kingdom by Lothair I. In 884 the Moorish pirates (Saracens) came over from Spain and settled in the mountains around Grimaud (Massif des Maures). They were expelled in 973, but they continued looting the coastal areas well into the 18th century.

Ancient ruins at Cimiez

In the 10th century feudalism was the prevalent form of rule. The Church had the greatest power. The cities proclaimed their independence. In the 12th century the Earldom of Provence fell into the hands of the Counts of Toulouse; after that to the Counts of Barcelona. In 1246 Provence went to the House of Anjou. In 1308 a Grimaldi purchased Monaco from the Genoans. Toward the middle of the 14th century, plague depopulated Europe. The southern coast of France was not spared from its ravages either.

After the death of the Queen of Sicily (revered as 'Pure Jeanne' by the people of Provence), the French House of Anjou and the King of Naples contended over who should rule Provence. Nice voted for the King of Naples, although he was not able to guarantee the city any effective protection. Count Amadeus VII from the Savoy exploited this situation. In 1388, he achieved his goal with the help of Johann Grimaldi, who then ruled Nice. This decision resulted in

13

Nice—with several interruptions—being in the possession of the Savoyards for five centuries. In contrast, the regions to the west of the Var remained a part of Provence and became French in 1486.

The area known in the present-day as the Côte d'Azur thus consisted of two sections from the Middle Ages into the 19th century. They belonged to different power blocs—which were also at enmity with each other. There were frequent violent confrontations. It was not until 1860 that the Earldom of Nice was finally incorporated into the State of France.

Monte Carlo

The First Tourists

The Monte Carlo Casino opened in 1878, and the previously rather insignificant region became the winter destination of kings and queens, aristocrats and politicians, courtesans, actors and actresses, musicians and artists. In 1887 the French poet Stephen Liègard entitled his book about France's Mediterranean coast *La Côte d'Azur*, thus giving the landscape its name forever.

'The azure-blue coast'... We think immediately of sun and sand, yachts and beaches, intense colours, mild nights and delicious scents, tanned skin and delights for the palate. It was not always thus, however; foreign visitors used to come for the autumn, winter and spring, since the summer sun of the Mediterranean coast was considered unhealthy. The British are especially convinced of this, and it was they who discovered and developed the Riviera. Cannes owes its present day fame to Lord Brougham, who settled there in 1834, and Queen Victoria—whose subjects had already financed the construction of the famous Promenade des Anglais in 1820—made Nice the 'Winter Capital of the British Empire' toward the end of the 19th century, at the same time St Tropez was being transformed into a painting centre by Paul Signac.

In Calais, where she landed with her yacht, Queen Victoria would join her private train, which 'raced' down to Nice at 35 miles (55km)

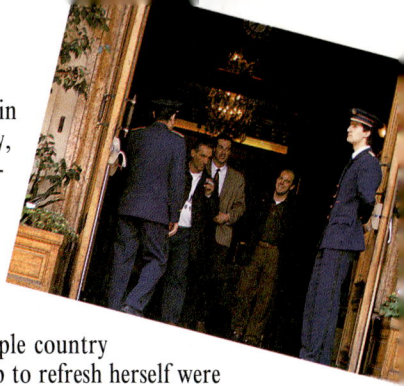

per hour. Her stay at the Hôtel Regina in Cimiez was the event of the year. Naturally, she entered the hotel through a private entrance exclusively reserved for her use, and she did not even have to forgo her own bed, which was brought in from London for the duration of her stay. Her special predilection was for touring the hinterland by coach. The proprietors of the simple country taverns and lodges in which she would stop to refresh herself were prepared for her arrival long ahead of time. Hastily painted and especially prominent signs were put up with the promise: "Five o'clock tea—any time of the day!"

The Belle Epoque lifestyle of the Côte d'Azur came to an end with World War I. The Royal Highnesses now had more important matters to attend to.

Between the Wars

The 1920s on the Côte d'Azur were the *annès folles*, wanton and wild, and long before Fellini coined the expression, the millionaires were living a very *Dolce Vita*. Cole Porter was one of the first to take up summer quarters in a villa on the Cap d'Antibes. It was thanks to him the rich American G Murphy and his wife Sara came in the *Train Bleu* from Paris to keep Porter company. In essence, this represented the beginning of the summer tourist industry on the Mediterranean coast.

In 1923, only one year later, the Murphys rented a villa on the Cape and introduced swimming and sunbathing. From then on bronzed skin, rather than pale, became the fashion order of the day, and aristocratic manners gave way to 'expensive simplicity'—still the only possible maxim for life on the Côte up to this day. Murphy and his attractive wife Sara gathered a clique around themselves every summer in their Villa America or the neighbouring houses. Its members included—amongst others—Hemingway, Picasso, Léger, the Mistinguetts and, perhaps predictably F Scott Fitzgerald and his wife Zelda.

André Sella was forced by his 'crazy' clientele to open the Hôtel du Cap in the summertime as well. (By the way, the hotel still looks

The Lêrins Islands

just as it did when Fitzgerald described it 60 years ago.) Once Sella was finally persuaded he adjusted quickly to the new conventions: for sun-worshippers and swimmers he built the Eden Roc pavilion next-door to his hotel. Erika Mann, the daughter of the Nobel prize-winner Thomas Mann (author of *The Magic Mountain*), later swooned: "It's a swimming pool such as one could scarcely find any-where else; carved into the cliffs so that it has something of a rather pathetic grotto; with diving boards at enormous heights—dizzying athletic equipment. The conditions of membership in this water sport club are very complicated and expensive. Above the swimming-bath there is a bar appointed in light green from which you can see noth-ing but the sea, so that you feel as if you're on a ship..."

At the same time a newly married couple appeared in Cannes on their honeymoon: Frank and Florence Gould. Florence, who left her native San Francisco after the 1906 earthquake, met her husband, a multi-millionaire and heir to a rail baron's estate, in Paris. On an outing the two discovered a pine grove and beach next to the little village of Juan-les-Pins. It was the famous *coup de foudre* which is reputed to have lasted for a lifetime. Florence not only bought all the land, she began to build on it immediately: first a casino and then the Hôtel Le Provençal, which was soon a serious rival to the Hôtel du Cap ("Oh, so distinguished" oozed the English advertising flyers). She also built a villa for herself and Frank which she trans-formed into a neo-Gothic castle. The Côte d'Azur has always inspired excess of one sort or another.

The Goulds received not only *le beau monde*, but also famed au-thors of the time. Benoit, Gide, Morand, Montherlant, Giraudoux, Louise de Vilmorin, Fitzgerald and his wife Zelda were, from 1924 on, among the guests who attended many wild and boisterous parties where the champagne flowed like a river. This was the decade of Gatsby abroad, the era immortalised in such books as Fitzgerald's *Tender is the Night*.

For more than half a century the Goulds ruled over Juan-les-Pins and Cannes, where they acquired Villa Le Patio. In rooms with splendid paintings on the walls ranging from Van Gogh to Matisse the stars of the Film Festival and other prominent people celebrated

with them: Sophia Loren, Ingrid Bergman, Picasso and Dali, Maurice Chevalier and Francoise Sagan, René Clair and Orson Welles, Elizabeth Taylor and Richard Burton. In 1961 General de Gaulle honoured Mrs Gould for meritorious patronage. She died in 1983 at 88 years of age.

Back to the year 1925. The famed Colette, of whom more anon, until then a convinced visitor of Bretagne, fell in love with St Tropez. There she discovered for the first time the pleasures of the *Midi*. The author of *Claudine in Paris*, and *Gigi* invited her friends to her house (La Treille Muscate, situated in the middle of a vineyard), and such distinguished names as Lucien Guitry, Dunoyer de Segonzac, Jean-Pierre Aumont, Jeff Kessel, Saint Exupéry, Cocteau, Simone Simon and Marc Allégret were visitors.

Who is the fairest on the beach?

Romance Blooms

In 1930 a tall and very slim young woman called Yvette, who lived in Cannes with her parents, was selected as 'Miss France'. Not far from the fashion salon in which Yvette worked, the Aga Khan—who frequently visited Cannes—was amusing himself playing skittles. The fateful meeting of the two did not take place on the Croisette, but rather eight years later in Cairo. Yvette became 'The Begum', one of the richest women in the world. The couple lived in Le Cannet in the Villa Yakimour—*Y* for Yvette, *mour* as in *amour!* There was scarcely a party on the Côte that the two didn't attend. After the death of her husband in 1957, Yvette largely abstained from the hubbub, dedicating herself to painting and sculpture. She is often still seen on the streets of Cannes, and in meeting her, some might

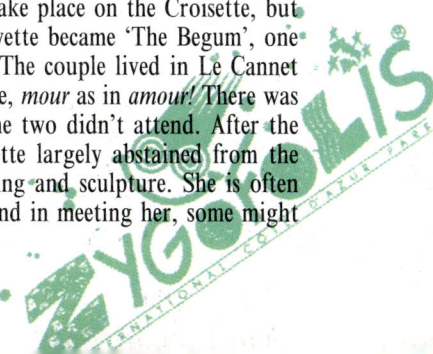

The Hôtel de Paris in Monte Carlo

reflect with melancholy on the wonderful days now gone.

In 1936, when the tourists and photographers were getting on her nerves, Colette sold her house in St Tropez. From then on, whenever she visited her beloved *Midi* she stayed with friends in Grasse or in the Hôtel de Paris in Monte Carlo.

In that December some 200 international journalists awaited the arrival of Wallis Simpson, an American woman who—as would soon be demonstrated—was worth more to a king than his throne. On 12 December, 1936 King Edward VIII abdicated, saying that he did not feel that he was able to fulfil his duties as monarch without the help and support of the woman he loved. With tears in her eyes the twice-divorced Wallis listened to this declaration of love in her Villa Viei. Six months later the couple were married. In the Château de la Croe on the Cap d'Antibes the Duke and Duchess of Windsor led a luxurious life in exile. At the beginning of World War II they left the Château, not returning until 1945.

War and After

The Italian past of the Earldom of Nice inspired Mussolini to bring the south-eastern tip of France 'home' to Italy. The Italians occupied Menton in 1940. As in World War I, this war resulted in the absence of guests on the Côte. After the split between Germany and Italy, German troops took over the occupation. The emigrants considered undesirables who remained were transported away via French camps to be brutally murdered; the French Resistance was likewise violently suppressed. In 1944 troops of the Allies liberated Provence. The era of Terror was over.

View of Menton

In 1946 Picasso came to Antibes and painted as if possessed. His large-scale work named *Joie de Vivre* said it all—the war was finally over, the pleasures of life were back. At the beginning of the 1950s Picasso busied himself intensively with the war theme. He transformed the Roman chapel in Vallauris into a monument to peace with his milestone work *La Guerre et la Paix* (War and Peace).

Picasso was not the only artist at work here in the 1950s. Matisse was working on the chapel in Vence; Chagall painted his *Messages Bibliques*. St Tropez—already in vogue among the literary circles of Paris—received its most famous resident: Brigitte Bardot. Before long the less pleasant consequences of her meteoric rise became apparent. Brigitte was no longer able to go for walks along the harbour or go shopping in the narrow alleyways of the town without being whistled at or harassed by tourists. They even showed up in boats in front of her villa La Madrague in order to get a glimpse of their idol or to take a photograph. Fatigued by her own mystique she even attempted suicide.

In Monaco, Rainier III prevailed against Onassis and orientated himself toward the American example—commercialising caviar and hot-dogs to the same degree. He also gained the support of a woman who gave up a successful film career for his sake. As Grace Kelly she was a major star in Hollywood; however, she played her biggest and best rôle in Monaco. The Prince of Monaco—from the land of big-time gambling—called the dice right with Princess Grace.

Modern Development

Since then, there is no doubt that the times and the Côte d'Azur have changed. The Promenade des Anglais is now a superhighway. Those who wish to visit St Tropez (and cannot afford to rent a helicopter) will get stuck for hours in the traffic jams. The railroad tracks no longer belong to the private trains of the upper crust, but rather to the fastest train in the western world: the TGV careens along at 170 miles (270km) per hour. Once it was the happy few who could afford the Côte; now it's approximately 18 million tourists who visit here annually.

Tourism has made the region famous, brought affluence, and defined its modern face. It's the basis of the economy. Business and congress 'tourism' is becoming ever more extensive: financially powerful groups fill hotel beds in the off-season as well.

In an attempt to avoid the monoculture of tourism the Côte has decided to encourage the establishment of 'clean' high-tech industry.

The Harbour at St Tropez

Recent projects which reflect this decision include the research centre of the American information-processing giant IBM in La Gaude and the ambitious project of the 'Innovation Park', Sophia Antipolis, near Valbonne.

Europe is becoming increasingly interested in the region. In the largest current project France is bringing natural gas into the area from Norway and is involved, to the tune of 6 billion francs, in the Europarc in Mougins. The opening of this facility is planned for 1993, and is expected to create some 7,000 new jobs. Another international project, 'Amadeus', unites four major airlines: Air France, Lufthansa, Iberia and SAS. The headquarters of this joint venture is at Sophia Antipolis.

Money is also being poured into luxury real-estate. The Villa Trianon on Cap Ferrat cost the late Christina Onassis 800,000 francs in rent per month. This piece of real estate is the property of the Vietnamese government and is on the market for 1.2 billion francs. The Fabris, Rizzolis and Mondadoris have bought into the Cap as well. Price per villa? Between 20 and 30 million US dollars. Because his Villa Estella seemed too small when compared to the Hôtel du Cap on the Cap d'Antibes, Greek tycoon John Latsis bought 40 additional acres (16 hectares) of land with buildings: among these were the Hôtel de la Residence du Cap, the Villa Soleil and L'Orangerie.

These few example should help to make clear what development has taken place in the region! Even so, there is more to the Côte d'Azur than the bravura of the coastal strip. Coast and hinterland are two extremes which nonetheless have a unity in their contrasts. It is precisely these contrasts which help transform a visit here into a unique experience. It doesn't matter how you define the word vacation—there's something for everyone here.

The Balls Keep Rolling

The call *Faites vos jeux! Rien ne va plus* was heard for the first time in Monaco in 1856. Many have succumbed to a fascination with the vagaries of the little tumbling ball. Some, from superstition, picked up a few cheap postcards in the shop opposite the Casino before coming in and 'inadvertently' stroking them over the owner's humped back (thought sure to bring good luck). When the 'humpback' died, he left behind a considerable fortune—including the humps—which hung from a chair on leather straps!

Churchill showed up in the casino for the first time in 1939. He returned in 1949, when (playing at the same table—at which nothing worth mentioning had happened in the meantime) he won 2 million francs while puffing away at his eternal cigar.

The balls are still rolling thanks particularly to wealthy Italian

Casinos

Cannes
CASINO DE LA CROISETTE
Tel: 93 38 45 00.
Opens 5pm. Admission 60FF.
CARLTON CASINO CLUB
Tel: 93 68 00 33. Opens 4pm.

St Maxime
CASINO
Tel: 94 96 12 96.
Open 9pm–5am.

Nice
CASINO RUHL
Tel: 93 87 95 87.
Open 5pm–4am (weekends and holidays until 5am). Also slot machines from 10am.

Monte Carlo
LOEWS CASINO
Tel: 93 50 65 00.
Open 1pm–5am.
CASINO DE MONTE CARLO
Tel: 93 50 75 75.
Salle Europe opens at noon. Admission 50FF; Salons Pouzet from 10pm; Salons Privés from 3pm; Café de Paris from 5pm; Slot machines from 10am.

Antibes/Juan-les-Pins
EDEN BEACH CASINO
Tel: 93 61 60 00.

La Napoule
CASINO DU LOEWS
Tel: 93 49 90 00
Open 8pm–4am. Slot machines 4pm.

guests from Turin and Milan. Meanwhile, one-armed bandits have also been installed. Tourists can try their luck on these in the afternoons—or even in the morning. Slot machines at such venues as the Casino Ruhl and casino de Monte Carlo open at 10am.

A little ball, called *le but* or *le bouchon*, also plays a considerable role in the most popular game of Southern France. In earlier days *boule* or *pétanque* was played with wooden balls sheathed with nails; nowadays they are made of stainless steel. One of the players throws the smallest ball—the wooden *bouchon*, which is about 1in (25mm) in diameter—for a distance of up to 60ft (20m). With the next throw he tries to get his metal ball as close as he possibly can to the *bouchon*.

A player of the other team then strives to get his ball still closer. The opponents take turns in their endeavours. For each ball which is closer than that of the best of the opposing team, the player receives one point. The game is finished when one team has 15 points. The challenge of the game lies, in part, in the various techniques for manoeuvering a ball closer to the *bouchon*. You can roll the ball directly towards the little wooden ball, or you can shoot for an enemy ball to push it away from the *bouchon*. Finally, you can aim at the *bouchon* to push it away from an enemy ball or bring it closer to one of your own.

The game is dominated by the decisions which a player must make before each toss: Should you aim? If yes, how? Is the terrain hard and fast or soft and slow? Are there irregularities and small stones on the track which could influence the course of the ball? A tremendous number of such questions and the expected result of a toss are amply discussed. In essence, this is the attraction of the game—especially for the spectator. The perspicacity, humour, sarcasm, insults, arguments and curses with which the individual players dramatise any given situation—and hopefully outfox their opponents are all part of the game of *boule*. And the hollow, deep thwack of one ball hitting another is one of the most unforgettable sounds of a summer evening on the Côte d'Azur.

22

From Bréa to César

The Nice School flourished between 1450 and 1570, a style of painting which can be compared in significance with that of Siena. The works of these painters—who were primarily in the employment of the Order of Penitent Monks—can be found in many of the pilgrimage churches and chapels in and around Nice; for example in Peille, Biot, Tourette-sur-Loup, Bar-sur Loup, Bouyon and Le Broc. The paintings and the buildings they ornament represent a lesser known facet of life on the Azure coast, a sort of counterpoint for the purely sybaritic pleasures of sunning and dining.

The best known painter of altar images and frescoes from this period was Louis Bréa. He was born in Nice and was called the 'Provençal Fra Angelico', probably because of the naïve uprightness, sincerity, humanity and simplicity with which he imbued his subjects. His brother Antoine, nephew François, Jean Miralheti, Jacques Durandi, Jean Canavesio, Jean Baleison and André de la Cella also belonged to *les primitifs niçois*.

In the 1950s and 1960s a Second School of Nice came into being. Among its members are Arman, Ben, Chubac, Farhi, Gilly, Klein, Malaval, Morabito, Slobodan, Sosno and César.

Forest Fires

In the south of France—the so-called *Midi*—fire is the feared enemy of the forests. Most of the perpetrators can't be taken to court: they include the heat of summer, dryness, coniferous woods and underbrush, the unpredictable *Mistral*, carelessness and lack of investment in preventative measures. Added to this, however, is indeed a criminal aspect: some 'people' start fires to benefit from insurance and some simply enjoy lighting fires.

Between 1985 and 1988 in the six *départments* of the Provence/Côtes d'Azur there were eight deaths and 130 people were injured in fires. In the *Midi* there are more than 10 million acres (4 million hectares) of forest and underbrush which require protection. Attempts are being made to reduce the danger of fire:

underbrush is being cleared around residential areas and houses, fire breaks are being cut through the forest and patrols have been established for the early detection of fires.

Fire fighting is carried out by the water-bombers of Canadair, who are stationed in Marignane. The 'flying fire-department' logs somewhere in the region of 7,000 hours flying time during the summer season, and the carefully chosen pilots risk their lives anew every day. They are masters of fire-fighting technique and are able to unload their water tanks at a height of only 100ft (30m) above ground level.

The 'Angels of the Forest' are a group of young men—green-helmeted and equipped with walkie-talkies—who cover about 125 miles (200km) a day on motorcycles in endangered areas. Their mission is the early detection of fires and the observation of visitors in the forest. The devastating spread of a forest fire can usually be prevented if the fire department can be called to the scene within the first 10 minutes. Since the establishment of the 'Green Helmets', pyromaniacs have not had such an easy time. But fire is now one of the greatest dangers throughout the entire mediterranean basin, and visitors are advised to keep that in mind.

RF

HOTEL DEVILLE

Il y a une jeunesse mystérieuse dans les plus vieilles pierres de St Jean. Cette jeunesse du pêcheur de bronze, accroupi sous les lauriers roses du port, et qui la symbolise.

Jean Cocteau citoyen d'honneur de St Jean 1961

Tour S...

The region covered by this guide is bordered by Menton in the east and St Tropez in the west. For the best overview of the area, use Michelin map 195.

Nice has been chosen as the point of departure for our trip because it is the capital city of the Côte d'Azur, as well as being the location of the international airport (the second-largest in France). Not by chance has this city become a major tourist centre and a gold mine for those seeking big-city diversions and activities.

If you like the fashionable life, Monte Carlo—the gambling capital of Europe—provides a unique milieu. Understated elegance awaits the visitors of Beaulieu, Cap Ferrat, Cap Martin and Menton—towns located along the coastal road, the Basse Corniche. You can also reach Menton from Nice via the Moyenne Corniche, which has magnificent views over the sea and the coastal villages and is, moreover, the quickest route to Eze, one of the region's best preserved mediaeval mountain villages. Those interested in history might prefer the Grande Corniche, which partly follows the course of the ancient Via Julia Augusta, and gives you the chance to visit Roquebrune (a fortified town from the Carolingian period) and the famous Roman victory monument, the Alpine Trophy.

The route from Nice to Vence leads us through hinterlands which have largely been spared from the hubbub of tourism. It also provides us the opportunity to see some of the original Provençe and—in Haut-des-Cagnes—saunter in the shade of Renoir's olive trees. Around Vence you can explore pure and charming landscapes and unspoiled mountain villages. Fame

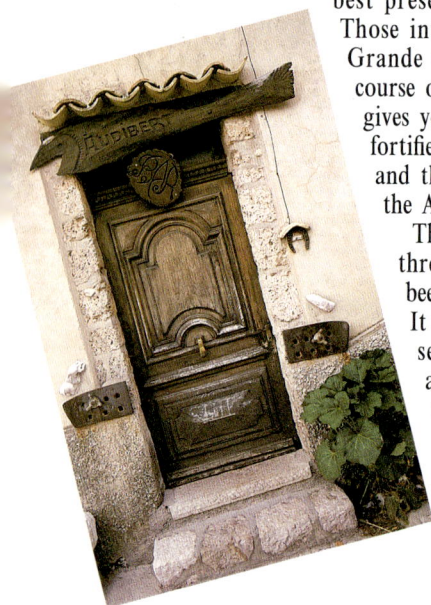

ections

has its price but, nonetheless, the modern art in the Fondation Maeght and a meal at the legendary Colombe d'Or are unforgettable.

The drive from Nice to Cannes offers an unbelievable number of possibilities: the Escoffier Museum in Villeneuve-Loubet, the Yacht and Picasso museums in Antibes, swimming and relaxation in the Cap d'Antibes, the night-life of Golfe Juan and Juan-les-Pins, ceramics wherever you cast your eye in Picasso's Vallauris, shopping in the glass-blowing workshop of Biot.

Next comes Cannes, the oasis of international high-society, an

Eldorado for gourmets, with its festival atmosphere, yacht-mania and starlets as well as the seductive aroma of the *cuisine provençale*. From here you can make an excursion out to the Lêrins Islands, or you can follow in the tracks of Napoleon through Mougins (with its renowned restaurants) to the perfume centre of Grasse.

After Cannes, the uniquely beautiful landscape of the Corniche de L'Esterel begins: red cliffs of volcanic stone, indented capes and little bays, swimming beaches and yacht harbours. Located along this stretch is St Raphael, which was once described as a 'stately, old-fashioned Riviera town'; right next to it is Fréjus, on the Via Aurelia. Those interested in history should definitely not miss the 'Roman City' and the mediaeval cathedral quarter.

Nice

The *Grande Dame* of the Riviera

The Promenade des Anglais; ice cream in the Hôtel Negresco; The Carré d'As and luxury boutiques, the heart of Nice, onion pie at Hélène's; the harbour, the high-priced quarter of Cimiez and the Chagall Museum (a whole day of sightseeing).

Nikaia, Nice, Nissa la Bella or simply *L'Olive*—the somewhat filled-out *Grande Dame* of the Riviera (with 350,000 inhabitants), swimming with memories of the days of crinoline, empresses (Eugénie) and queens (Victoria)—presses itself lasciviously against the sea. The **Promenade des Anglais**—so named because the English financed its construction—follows along the gentle curve of the Baie des Anges—the bay of Angels. Despite the crush of traffic which has replaced the pedestrians who once sauntered along in the shade of the palms, the Promenade has still managed to keep something of its original splendour.

"If you would like to see the most beautiful land in the world, here it is." So wrote painter Pierre Auguste Renoir to Berthe Morisot, while simultaneously qualifying his praise: "In winter, of course, it occurs to me that it's more like some kind of hot-house into which people with fragile health take refuge." Here he is referring to a mistaken medical notion that the mild climate of the Côte would be especially therapeutic to people with lung complaints, an error which, well into the 19th century, misled many people into spending their winters here—or even settling permanently—often a fatal mistake. More caustically, De Maupassant called it: "...a hospital of the *monde*, death's waiting room, the blooming graveyard of Europe's high nobility."

It wasn't until the 20th century that Nice gradually began to free itself from one-sided dependence on tourism. Alongside the construction of the airport (1957)—the second-largest in France, the founding of the University (1965)—one of the country's best—a school of hotel management, a college for the creative arts and music, a centre for contemporary art and the Acropolis convention centre, numerous museums were established as well, making Nice second only to Paris in its significance as a French museum town.

Let's set out on the **Promenade des Anglais** to take in some interesting sights along the way. **The International Museum for Naïve (or Primitive) Art** is located on the Avenue Val Marie. It is the richest museum of its kind, with an inventory of some 6,000 paintings from 27 countries. The 300 works on permanent display, donated by the collector and art critic Jakovsky, are done full justice in the bright rooms of the castle.

At Avenue des Baumettes 33, the **Musée des Beaux Arts** beckons

Beauty in seclusion

you to pay a visit. Here the main theme is academic painting of the 19th century. Modern art is scarcely represented here, with the exception of the Dufy Collection, which is exhibited on a rotating schedule. Back on the Promenade we stroll on further to the famous **Hôtel Negresco**, a typical building of the Belle Epoque, where we might have an ice cream or some other light refreshment on the terrace before taking a look into the **Masséna Museum** at Rue de France 65, in which you can see the works of the earlier masters of Nice.

The **Palais de la Méditerranée**, constructed in the 1930s, is located directly on the shore-line promenade. A little further on is the **Jardin Albert I** with its fountains (designed by Volti) and an open-air stage. Across the way there is a mini-train which leaves every 20 minutes, from which you can see the flower market, the old city and the castle gardens. The Turin-style **Place Masséna** represents the centre of the city these days. In this quarter of the city 64 luxury boutiques have joined forces as the **Carré d'As** (you'll see the sign: *Bienvenue au Carré d'As*) and have made quality and outstanding service their motto. The **Avenue Jean-Médicin** opens onto the plaza. This is the plane-tree-shaded main business street, on which the large department stores (Galeries Lafayette) and shopping centres (Nice Etoile) are located. **Santazur** (No 11) gives information on half-day excursions which take place on Wednesday and Friday afternoons, including a tour of Nice and its various quarters, monuments, traditions and activities. The **Rue Masséna / Rue de France** is a pedestrian zone and has attractive terrace cafés and restaurants as well as shops.

Now we leave modern Nice and head for the old quarter and harbour. These are located on the other side of the Paillon mountain

which has now been bridged over by the **Acropolis** convention, performance and exhibition centre. The building is anchored in the river by five immense arches. Both the exterior and interior are inset with the works of contemporary artists (Volti, Vasarely, Arman, César and others), which harmonise well with the architecture. A new theatre and a museum of modern art complete this complex which links Nice new and old.

La Vieille Ville—called the *Babazouk* in the dialect of Nice—is the heart and soul of Nice, this city of the worker, the rich and poor but dignified. Here Nissa la Belle awaits those who are prepared for a gradual unfurling of charms for the eyes, the nose, and the palate. The quarter smells of everything that makes Provençal cuisine so delicious; here the alleys are narrow and houses tall; the façades are colourfully ornamented with flowers and laundry hung out to dry; here the hubbub of southern lands prevails all day, mixed with loud voices and happy laughter. In the Rue Beaumont **Hélène** has been making the best *pissaladières* for 50 years! A piece of this delicious onion pie will give you the energy you need to go on and see the rest of the old quarter.

Coming from the Acropolis (from which you can proceed through a number of gardens on down to the beach), we hike over to the **Place Garibaldi**, which is surrounded by houses with loggias. This plaza is named in memory of the famous freedom fighter Giuseppe Garibaldi (1807–82) who was born here. We continue to the **Eglise St Martin-St Augustin**, the oldest parish church, in which Garibaldi was baptised. On the opposite side of the street is a monument erected to the heroine Catherine Séguranes: with a knife and her skirt laced up high she fought against the Turks allied with Franz I. The famous fish-market takes place each morning on the **Place St Francois**. The **Palais Lascaris** is actually the only house in the old quarter which it is possible to tour. The wooden appointments of the pharmacy on the ground floor are particularly beautiful. Niccolò Paganini (1782–1840) lived and died at 23 **Rue de la Prefecture**. He was refused a Catholic burial, which led to probably the longest journey the poor 'devil's fiddler' ever took. He was buried four times in different places until 1896, when he was at last laid to rest in the new cemetery in Parma.

The **Cours Saleya** lies between the old city and the sea. In the 19th century it was the meeting place of the finer society of Old Nice; today it's the destination of all those who love markets. Except for Sunday afternoon and Monday there is a flower market; Monday is the flea market. Around noon the proprietors put tables and chairs on the street. Here things taste twice as good with the light breeze blowing in from the sea. Little houses crowded up

against each other and the former wharf arsenal of the Savoyan-Sardinian navy, named the **Galerie des Ponchettes**—these separate the marketplace from the sea, which you can make out through two arched gateways.

On the almost 300ft (92m) high citadel-mountain—still named **Château** even though there hasn't been a castle there for a long time, you can enjoy a splendid panoramic view. Although it is more comfortable to ascend by the lift, the fit among us climb up the stairs—or you can take it easy and stroll up from the Rue Ségurane along the winding path to the highest point. In the beautifully located cemetery which you pass on the way back down is the grave of the daughter of Consul Emil Jellinek. The name doesn't mean anything to you? Well, Jellinek won the Nice-Maganon rally in 1899 in a Daimler; he had christened the car after his daughter—Mercedes!

Lovers of antiques should go through the Rue C Ségurane towards the harbour, where there is always something going on. Yachts and fishing boats are moored here as well as excursion ships and boats which you can rent. In the outer harbour are the docks for the modern automobile ferries to Corsica. At the **Quai des Deux Emmanuels** is the renowned, though not exactly cheap, gourmet spot **L'Esquinade**, which has kept its clientele loyal for some 30 years. Right in the area at Boulevard Carnot 27 is the **Musée Terra Amata**. The prehistoric finds exhibited there are proof that Nice was already inhabited 400,000 years ago.

Cimiez (the Roman *Cemenelum*) can be best reached via the Boulevard de Cimiez, the route also taken by the coaches of the Belle Epoque when the guests of the Winter Palace and the Hotels Ermitage, Alhambra and Regina returned from the sea back up to their hill. In the 1st century BC, after the conquest of the Maritime Alps, which represented an important passage to Gaul and Spain, the Romans constructed the Via Julia Augusta along the coast, and on the hills of Cimiez they erected their own town of Cemenelum, intended to rival the existing town of Nikaia. Some interesting things to see include the remains of villas and the arenas as well as the numerous finds in the **Musée d'Archélogie**.

At the **Place du Monastère** you will find the entrance to the cemetery where the painters Raoul Dufy (1877–1953) and Henri Matisse (1869–1954) and the writer Martin du Gard are buried. The **Musée Matisse** in the Avenue des Arènas displays the development of this versatile artist with paintings, drawings, prints, and bronze figures. Matisse, who also designed the chapel in Vence, lived in Nice for 20 years, lastly in the Hôtel Regina, the very one which was built for Queen Victoria. On the way back you should by no means miss your chance to see the **Chagall Museum** (Avenue Dr Ménard), a flat, modern structure of concrete and glass which was specially conceived by Hermant for the painter Marc Chagall's *Messages Bibliques*.

Carneval (Carnival)

Carneval (beginning three weeks before Shrove Tuesday) is Nice's largest and most famous festival. The costumed parade was already established by 1848, when it often degenerated into a chalk and flour battle. In 1873, festival floats appeared for the first time and shortly thereafter came the figures and caricatures. The parades and flower battles which occur today and the incineration of the float of 'King Carneval', accompanied by a big fireworks display, attract visitors from all over the world.

The **Festival des Cougourdons** in March is a big folk festival which takes place in the gardens of the Arenas of Cimiez. The **Fêtes des Mais**, also held in Cimiez on the four Sundays of the month of May, are a delightful combination of evening dances, picnics on the green, folk-dancing and other folklore presentations.

Restaurants

Reasonable (Under 100FF)
AU SOLEIL
7 rue d'Italie.
Tel: 93 88 77 74.

LA NISSA SOCCA
5, rue St. Réparate.
Tel: 93 80 18 35.
LA MEREANDA
4, rue de la Terrane.
Closed Saturday evening, Sunday and Monday in February and August (no telephone).

Expensive
LES DENTS DE LA MER
2 rue St François de Paule.
Tel: 93 80 99 16.
L'ESQUINADE
5 quai Deux-Emmanuels.
Tel: 93 89 59 36.
LE CHANTECLER
37 promenade des Anglais, in the Hôtel Negresco. Tel: 93 88 39 51.

Accommodation

Reasonable
HOTEL ALFA
30 rue Masséua. Tel: 93 87 88 83
HOTEL LES CIGOGNES
16 rue Maccaram. Tel: 93 88 65 02.
NOUVEL HOTEL
19 boulevard Victor Hugo.
Tel: 93 84 86 85.
HOTEL RIVOLI
47 rue Pastorelli. Tel: 93 62 17 84.
RELAIS CIMIEZ
128 boulevard de Cimiez.
Tel: 93 81 18 65

Nice→L

In order to get from Nice to Menton (or vice-versa) there are three alternatives: for coastline fans there's the Basse Corniche (unfortunately heavily travelled); for speed enthusiasts there's the Moyenne Corniche and for nature and picnicking, the Grande Corniche.

Basse Corniche

The Coastal Road N98

The city of Villefranche; the mediaeval Rue Obscure; fish in La Mère Germain; the Peninsula of the Billionaires; a walk around the cape; panorama from the lighthouse; St Jean Cap Ferrat (Nice–Menton 20 miles [31km]; with sightseeing half a day).

"At this place between heaven and earth the world stands still." So Maurice Maeterlinck (winner of the 1911 Nobel Prize for Literature) described the white-ochre palace—with which he fell im-

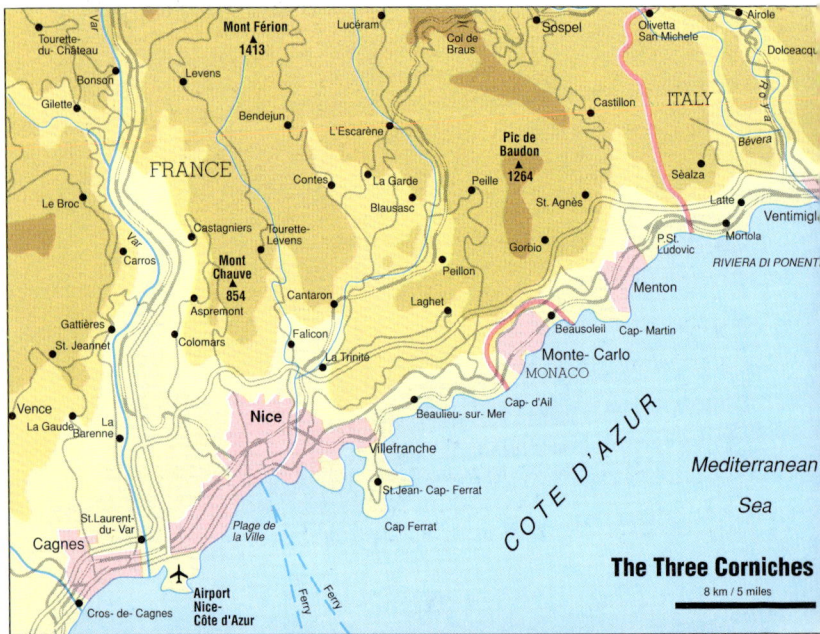

The Three Corniches

8 km / 5 miles

mediately in love—in his work *Les Sept Fées d'Orlamondé*. Today it houses the exclusive Club Bonmont Mélisande. The invitation of a member is something I would not turn down, even if only for the the unique view from its terrace. It is located on the way out of Nice in the direction of Menton (Information: 30 Blvd Maeterlinck; Tel: 93 56 21 12).

Villefranche (Free City) is on one of the most beautiful inlets on the Mediterranean. Where the yachts and sporting boats set anchor today there was once a naval port in which galleys were constructed and in whose deep waters the King of France reluctantly went swimming in 1538. The tall, colourful façades of the old

quarter hem the attractive **fishing harbour**. The picturesque tangle of narrow alleyways—partly constructed with steps and arching over the peculiar **Rue Obscure**—still look positively mediaeval.

Right in the heart of the neighbourhood is the **Chapelle St Pierre**, which was given stained-glass windows by Jean Cocteau in 1957. Beginning in the 1920s he stayed in a wide variety of places on the Côte. The **Hôtel Welcome**, in which he lived from time to time, still exists today and is thoroughly recommended.

The imposing **Citadel**, erected at the end of the 16th century for the protection of the bay, shelters the **Goetz-Boumeester Museum**, primarily displaying abstract paintings as well as works of Picasso,

Miró and Hartung. The same complex houses the **Volti Museum**, dedicated to native artists. It features sculptures of female figures whose setting—in the large courtyard of the citadel—does them full justice.

The **Institute de Français** (23 Avenue Général Leclerc; Tel: 93 01 88 44), located in a villa a little way above the harbour offers well-to-do fans of learning, four-week-long intensive French courses. Starting at 5pm, Institute students meet at **Chez Betty**; lone travellers can make some international acquaintances here. The excellent fish dishes of the **La Mère Germain** were prized by Cocteau. From the Pont St Jean you can take an outing to the Cap Ferrat—called the "Peninsula of Billionaires"—and not just because of cost of the villas. Each has its own history—hidden in a park-like estate characterised by bombastic, not to say peculiar, architecture. Among the largest are the Maryland, La Vigiè, Mes Roches and Serena—all located on the **Plage Passable**, a sandy beach which slopes gently down to the sea.

Somerset Maugham lived in the Villa Mauresquè; Edith Piaf and Jean Marais resided in the Villa Sospiro. The property of the Rothschilds has gone to the state, and Les Cédres, the 35 acres (14ha) property of King Leopold II of Belgium, is divided today between the liqueur dynasty of Marnier-Lapostolle, Italy's most powerful automobile producer, and a zoo whose 'Chimpanzee School' is great fun for children.

The beauty and quiet of the peninsula has been preserved thanks to these villas—the mute witnesses of a lustrous epoch gone by. Even the *nouveau riche*—whose mostly unoccupied villas are surrounded by dogs and heavily armed bodyguards—haven't been able to destroy the charm of the peninsula. Behind the zoo there is a road leading steeply down to the sea; from there you can take a walk around the cape on the former customs road. Along the way you will find small and uncrowded swimming inlets. A splendid view awaits the coura-

geous among you who don't shy away from ascending the 164 steps to the lighthouse—one of the most modern in France. At the tip of the peninsula is a tower which served as a jail in the 18th century. At the end of the path which passes it is the **Chapelle St Hospice**; next to it a gigantic Madonna statue.

The **Musée Ile-de-France**, an Italian-style palace which the Baroness Ephrussi de Rothschild had built at the beginning of the 20th century to house her art collection, is particularly worth visiting because of its splendid gardens (open daily except Monday from July 1–August 31 from 3–9pm; from September 1–June 30 from 2–6pm).

St Jean Cap Ferrat, with its harbour and several well-preserved old houses, has—despite modernization—managed to hold onto its picturesque charm.

Beaulieu, located on the Baie des Fourmis, is among the warmest places on the French Riviera—a luxurious oasis of quiet for the well-to-do and casino fans. Somewhat more affordable, on the other hand, is the mouth-watering seafood gratin at the **L'African Queen** at the Port de Plaisance. The fish-stews or mini-bouillabaises at the **Key Largo** are also delicious.

The **Villa Kérylos** is worth a visit because of its beautiful park (open July and August from 3–7pm, otherwise from 2–6pm). For those who want to walk after lunch, there are two good routes: the **Maurice Rouvier Promenade** follows along the sea up to St Jean Cap Ferrat and the round trip takes about one hour; the footpath to the **Plateau St Michel** and back can be covered at a brisk pace in an hour and a half.

Head next for **Eze Bord de Mer**, from where you can climb up to Eze Village by foot—as did Nietzsche as he conceived of the third part of *Thus Spake Zarathustra*. Then by way of the Cap d'Ail, whose beautiful villas are hidden among firs, palms and cypresses on the lower cliffs of the Têtes de Chien (a cliff in the form of a dog's head) we reach the Principality of Monaco.

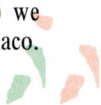

Monaco

Caviar and Hot Dogs

The Old City: from the Cathedral to the Palace of Justice; Musée Oceanographique; the plaza before the castle and the Palais Princier; Parc Paysager and the rose garden; tips for Monte Carlo by day and night (half a day).

The Grimaldis had their main seats in Cagnes, Beuil, Naples and Genoa. Francesco Grimaldi, driven out of Genoa, took control of Monaco in 1297 in a coup in which he and his assistants disguised themselves as monks. He was not able to hold Monaco, but even to this day the armed monk in the Grimaldi coat of arms is a reminder of this coup. In the year 1308 another Grimaldi bought Monaco from the Genoans.

The history of this principality is fraught with family strife—in which one murder more or less didn't matter much—as well as oc-

Monaco
320 m / 0.2 miles

Homes of the rich and famous

cupation by various foreign powers. In 1861 the principality became smaller as a result of the loss of the towns of Roquebrune and Menton, which were incorporated into France, and the financial misery of the principality, which was already acute, was made worse. Accordingly, Charles III allowed gambling, which was forbidden in the neighbouring countries, eliminated direct taxation and, in 1862, had a small casino constructed in Monte Carlo. His hope that these measures would enable him to overcome his financial problems was not fulfilled—at first.

The situation changed when François Blanc became the licensed proprietor of the casino and with several partners organized the **Société des Bains de Mer** (SBM). Before long a new city came into existence around the casino, with palatial hotels, villas and magnificent grounds. Towards the end of the 19th century the rich guests finally appeared—although only in winter at first. Today there are several million visitors a year. If Aristotle Onassis (for a period the controlling stockholder of the SBM) had followed through with his wishes, Monaco today would be the exclusive enclave of the super-rich.

Rainer III, however, was of a different mind. In the 1950s he adopted American-style marketing, aimed at making Monaco appeal to ordinary visitors as well as the rich. In the meantime the SBM has grown into a gigantic enterprise, whose restaurants have accumulated a total of five Michelin stars. The **Louis V** owes three of them to their Chef Ducasse; his student Caironi has conquered one for the Grill des Hôtel de Paris; while Garnier in La Coupole des Hôtel Mirabeau has had his for some time.

In addition the tax-paradise is a seductive destination for top earners. Indeed, the Prince has only accepted 4,000 applications for citizenship in the last 15 years. To name just a few of the privileged persons: Boris Becker, Alain Prost and best-selling authors

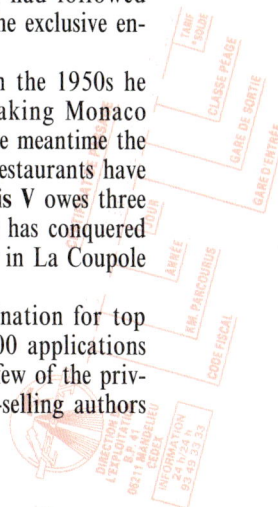

Eldorado for boat fans

such as Simmel and Anthony Burgess. Burgess has been punching the keys of his old Remington here for the last 15 years. He loves it just as much as his old piano, which once belonged to Josephine Baker. Burgess took refuge in the safety of Monaco because the Mafia had threatened to kidnap his son.

The 33,559 inhabitants of the principality—of which only 4,500 are 'real' citizens of Monaco—live in total security. The video observation system is just as discreet as it is effective, and it's practically unique in the world. Fifty cameras observe the 'weak points' of the city day and night. In addition there are 400 police officers with modern equipment; they are further supported by 200 civilian security officers. It is no wonder that you see so many luxury yachts, expensive automobiles, *haute-couture* clothing and precious jewellery here. In Monaco you can show what you own without danger.

The tiny principality includes the old city of Monaco on the cliffs (Le Rocher), Monte Carlo—the newer section of the city—with the business and harbour quarter, La Condamine, between the two, and the Fontvieille quarter below the botanical gardens. Monaco, the 'capital' of this miniature state, is located on a cliff 1,000ft (300m) wide by 2,600ft (800m) long, which extends out to sea. In the **Cathedral** there are several altar paintings by Louis Bréa and plaque paintings of the Nice School. The **Old City** is located between the Cathedral and the Palace of Justice. In its alleyways you can listen to Les Petits Chanteurs de Monaco each Sunday around 10am (in summer), as they sing mass in the Cathedral.

Guillaume Apollinaire passed through the shaded alleys of the **Jardin St Martin**; the **Placette Bosio** commemorates this French poet. The members of the Grimaldi dynasty are immortalised as waxen figures in the **Historial des Princes de Monaco**, which is located on one the Rue Basse (one of the most beautiful streets in the old quarter).

At the monumental **Musée Oceanographique** it's not difficult to see why it took 11 years to build. Its aquarium, with more than 90 tanks, is certainly among the most interesting in Europe. The citizens of Monaco have Albert I, whose passion for research led him on many sea voyages, to thank for this museum dedicated to oceanography.

Just a short hop from here you can experience the **Monte Carlo Story** in close up in the form of a multi-vision spectacle. The **Plaza before the Castle** lends the cannons and cannonballs—a gift from Louis XIV—something of an operatic air. This impression is strengthened by the changing of the guard, which takes place every day punctually at 11.55am.

The view from the parapet is truly dream-like: you see the harbour, Monte Carlo, the coast out to the point of Bordighera, the city quarter of Fontvieille and the Cap d'Ail. **Le Palais du Prince** can be toured in part; sheltered in one of its wings is an interesting museum for fans of Napoleon. There is an open-air

View of two harbours

theatre with seating for 350 in the Fortresse, built at the beginning of the 18th century on the north-easternmost point of the Rocher.

Cactus lovers are advised to go and see the **Jardin Exotique**—there are 7,000 different species here. The huge **Stadium Louis II** was dedicated in 1985 and fits in well with the architecture of the new **Fontvieille** quarter. The unfinished **Parc Paysager** is a green oasis of peace amid all the skyscrapers with its freshwater lake, on which ducks and swans swim and feed. In the neighbouring **Rose Garden** there are 3,500 varieties of this noble flower to admire.

Exclusivity, the exotic, extravagance, luxury and a passion for gambling: all this is **Monte Carlo**. While outsiders wander stunned and gaping from Rolls to Rolls and pay homage to the one-armed bandits in the outer hall of the Casino (from 10am), the insiders entertain themselves in the **Monte Carlo Sporting** or the **Old Beach Club** and go shopping in the **Rue Grimaldi** or the **Metropol**.

The *hoi polloi*—as well as those with a sense of self-respect—might take their lunch in the **Café de Paris**; dine in the evening at **Rampoldi** (my favourite place for Italian specialities,) or in the **Louis XV**, or possibly in the **Pinocchio**, the **Pulcinella**, the **Off-shore** or

Seeing—and being seen

the **Sans Souci**, and afterwards go dancing until the grey light of dawn at **Jimmy's** or in the **Livingroom**—without abstaining first of all from an excursion into **Snooker's Bar**, the **Sao Brazil** or **La Réserve**. And, naturally, one does not stop at the *Machines à sous*, for which you only need coins; rather you lay out the bills on the roulette tables of the **Salons Touzet** or the **Salons Privés**. It is to be hoped that you are spared the misfortunes of the beautiful Oteros, who lost in one single night all that she had earned on her triumphant tour of the United States.

Outstanding opera, theatre, ballet and concerts are presented in Carles Garnier's **Little Opera**, which also has theatre boxes for royalty. On the south side of the casino—providing, of course, that it's the right time of day—there are sun-flooded terraces from which you can get a delightful view. A colourful work in *lavaemaille* by Vasarély decorates the roof of the Congress Auditorium.

Right on the sea, in the Avenue Princess Grace, a villa built by Garnier houses what is quite probably the most interesting museum in Monaco: the **Musée de Poupées et Automates**. It houses a collection of over 100 automatons—set in motion several times daily—as well as a collection of puppets that was started in the 18th century and includes a Neapolitan nativity scene.

If you enjoy walking, there is a beautiful path which leads from Monte Carlo Beach to the Cap Martin and another from Fontvieille to Cap d'Ail.

Special Events

January: Rallye Automobile de Monte Carlo.
February: International TV Festival
April: International Tennis.
May: Grand Prix Automobile.
June: International Golf.
July/August: Concert in the castle courtyard and fireworks festival.
19 November: Monaco's national holiday.
December: Circus festival.

Restaurants

Reasonable

LE ST PIERRE
Rue de la Turbie. Tel: 93 30 99 96.

LES DEUX GUITARES
Rue de la Colle. Tel: 93 30 16 30.

BACCUS
Rue de la Turbie. Tel: 93 30 19 35.

Expensive

HOTEL DE PARIS
Tel: 93 50 80 80.
Le Louis XV. Closed Tuesday and Wednesday, except from 15 June to 15 September. Closed completely from 28 February–15 March. Complete menus 500–580FF; à la carte 700FF.
Le Grill. Complete menu 300FF; à la carte 500FF.
La Salle Empire. A la carte.
Terasse de la Salle Empire. From June to September; à la carte.

HOTEL HERMITAGE
La Belle Epoque. Tel: 93 50 80 80/ 50 67 31. Daily menu 270FF.
Terrasse de la Belle Epoque. Open July–August.

HOTEL MIRABEAU
Tel: 93 50 80 80/50 80 93
La Coupole. Closed Wednesday. Complete menus 225–340FF; à la carte 400FF.
Am Pool. Open from June–September. Lunch and dinner; strictly à la carte.

MONTE CARLO BEACH
Tel: 93 78 21 40.
La Potinière. Open from June–mid-September. A la carte and diet menu.
Le Rivage. A la carte.
La Vigie. Open July–August. Buffet 230FF.

CAFÉ DE PARIS
Tel: 93 50 57 75.
Open year-round from 8am–5am. Offers both complete menus and à la carte.

LA PISCINE DES TERRASSES
Tel.: 93 30 22 55. A la carte and diet menu.

LE CASINO
Le train bleu. Tel: 93 50 69 31. A la carte daily specials.
Le Cabaret. Tel: 93 50 80 80. From mid September–June. A la carte and complete menus 360FF.
Le Privé. Tel: 93 50 69 31. From mid September–June. A la carte.

MONTE CARLO SPORTING CLUB
Salles des étoiles. Tel: 93 50 80 80. Dining, show and dancing from the end of June–mid-September. Complete menus: 420, 600 & 750FF.
Maona. Tel: 93 30 71 71. Dinner from end of June–mid-September Complete menus 350FF.
Maona Fuji. Tel: 93 30 71 71. Dinner from end of June–mid-September. Complete menus 350FF.
Roger Vergé Café. Tel: 93 25 86 12. Closed Sunday. Complete menus 90–110FF; à la carte 220FF.
Terrasses Saint-James. Tel: 93 25 86 12. Daily specials and à la carte.

Affordable Accommodation

HOTEL DE FRANCE
Tel: 93 30 24 64.
Next to the train station.
HOTEL DE L'ETOIL
Tel: 93 30 73 924.
Rue des Oliviers.
HOTEL TERMINUS
Tel: 93 30 20 709.

Menton

Entertainment, beaches, a generous cultural selection; the pedestrian zone Rue St Michel; Palais Carnolès; the view from the Jardin des Colombières; excursions to villages, monasteries and markets starting from Menton.

The harbour at Menton

With 300 sunny days per year and the protection of mountain terraces covered with forests or citrus and olive groves, **Menton** is considered a real pearl of the Côte d'Azur. It also has one of its warmest climates. In addition there's a casino, countless restaurants, nightclubs, yacht harbours and endless sandy beaches.

What makes the city *really* special, however, is the maxim of the city leaders—to offer its citizens and visitors an array of impressive cultural events: concerts, museums, exhibitions, a theatre season from November to April, the **Lemon Festival** in February, flower festivals in summer with magnificent parades, festive evenings in the **Parc du Pian**, a circle of poets and the award of the **Katherine Mansfield Prize** for the best novel (the New Zealand-born author passed some time in Menton around the turn of the century).

The well-known chamber music festival performances which the Hungarian-born André Borocz brought to life some 40 years ago are especially worthy of mention. Borocz's hatred of ants drove him to despair on his vacation in Juan-les-Pins, moving him to take quarters with friends in Menton where, on a beautiful August evening, he discovered the Italianate plaza of St Michael's Church; the sound of Haifitz playing a Bach violin concerto drifted out of an open window and created an acoustic backdrop for the sunset. Needless to say, Borocz was moved by this serendipitus weaving of

elements, and sought to reproduce the experience for others. The intimate plaza creates a unique setting for the festival performances: the ochre of the largest and most beautiful Baroque church in the area, the rose hue of the adjacent chapel; grey and white cobblestones arranged into the Grimaldi coat of arms—and a ceiling of glowing stars.

There is a wedding chamber embellished by Jean Cocteau located in the City Hall, and in the little 17th-century fort is a **Museum** in honour of this multi-media artist, who died in 1963. The **Rue Longue** follows the Via Julia Augusta—the former main traffic artery; the **Rue Michel** with its little orange trees is a pedestrian zone. To the left below it is the gravel-paved **Place aux Herbes**, and not far from there are the **Market Halls**—in which you can't help but buy *something*.

The **Jardin Biovés** was built right over the Carei River, which is in full spate in the spring. With its tall palms, citrus trees, fountains and statues, the garden is the centre of February's Lemon Festival. The 18th-century **Palais Carnolés**, the former residence of the Prince of Monaco, stands in a beautiful park and looks very Italian. The abundant art collection in the palace is well worth seeing. In the **Jardin Botanique** 700 plant species thrive as a result of the ideal climate.

The best general views are to be had from the old **cemetery**. Another beautiful view over the rising arcades of Old Menton with its high, narrow houses before a mountain backdrop is found among the pines and cypress of the **Jardin des Colombières**, which were laid out by the author and architect Ferdinand Bac. Unfortunately, it is not that easy to find good food in Menton. My recommendation is: **Chez Germaine**, 46 Promenade du Maréchal Leclerc; Tel: 93 35 66 90; menus from 90–150FF.

There are numerous possible outings to be made from Menton. You might venture out to **Gorbio** (D23) or **St Agnès** (D22) for example, two mountain villages of a kind which won't be around much longer. Or you may perhaps choose to drive via the D2566 to the monastery **L'Annonciade**, a destination of pilgrims since the 11th century. There is, as well, the **Forêt de Menton**, a mixed forest which is a pleasant place to go for a hike up to **Col de Castillon**, through **Sospel** and back to the coast. Or, on Fridays, you may choose to visit **Ventimiglia**, which is renowned for its market.

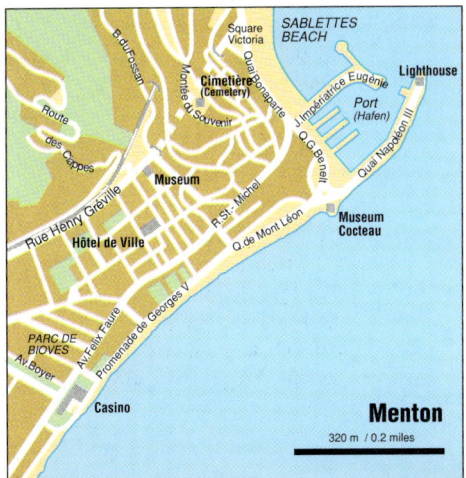

Pleasures for the Palate

Eze Village; the ruins of the Saracen fortress with a view over the entire Riviera; dining in the Château Eza or in the Chevre d'Or; the exclusive residential area of Cap Martin on the Peninsula (Nice–Menton 20 miles [31km]; half a day).

The broad and well improved N7 road leads us, by the fastest route, to **Eze Village**. We won't be the only ones who pass through the gate of the old Saracen fortress on the Avenue du Jardin Exotique, or who follow the Rue de Brec up to the church with its baroque interior.

After the Rue de la Paix comes the Rue du Château with its dark archways, then we climb up the stairs to the **Jardin Exotique** at the highest point of the conical hill. At the ruins of the fortress, destroyed by order of Louis XIV, we are 1,407ft (429m) above sea level and can sweep our view across the entire Riviera. On our return path we should examine the **Chapelle des Pénitents Blancs**, a simple building from the 14th century whose external walls are ornamented with enamel paintings.

At the end of the Rue de la Pise there is the **Moorish Gateway** to our right and on the left the former residence of Prince William of Sweden. The **Château Eza** (Tel: 93 41 12 24) houses a hotel and restaurant to satisfy the most demanding clientele; the **Chèvre d'Or** is a second gourmet temple (Tel: 93 41 12 12) in the Rue du Barri. You should definitely stop off at one of these two restaurants—but not without having reserved a table. Dining here cannot be described as inexpensive—but it is a unique experience.

Past Eze the Corniche continues around the Tête de Chien and then runs above the Principality of Monaco (see Route 3). If we remain on the N7 we go around Monaco and arrive at **Beausoleil**, which nestles into the south cliffs of the Mont des Mules. After that the Corniche leads us on past the Vista Palace and joins the coastal road at Cabbé. The modern seaside resort of **Roquebrune** is located down the mountain from the village of Roquebrune (see Tour 6).

Cap Martin is the fanciest neighbourhood of Menton. On this peninsula, which is overgrown with olive groves, cypresses, mimosas and pine woods, there are splendid villas and grounds. Their well-to-do owners are no doubt pleased by the fact that there isn't much else for tourists to look at.

The mild climate, gentle air and flourishing vegetation have always pleased those able to afford to live here. The beautiful Sissi of Austria loved the South and the sea above all; Eugénie, the French Empress, hoped for an improvement of her illness whilst staying here; King Umberto of Italy, Churchill, Le Corbusier and the Chanels came here because of the peace and quiet.

The 'immortal' Garbo—always on the run—hid herself here in the splendidly located estate of the Russian Princess Anna Chervachidzé, which today belongs to the Lebanese billionaire Hani Salaam. Silvano Mangano and the Italian film producer Dino de Laurentiis have frequently tarried here in the residence Casa del Mare, which is located very close by.

You can take a beautiful walk from the point of the cape up to Monte Carlo Beach.

The Cannes coast

Grande Corniche

Dining in La Ferme St Michel; Col d'Eze with a view over the high mountain valleys of Vésubie and Var; the Trophée des Alpes and the Roquebrune village (half a day).

Napoleon ordered the construction of this uppermost Corniche, which partly follows the course of the Roman Via Julia Augusta. The **Nice Observatory** (Boulevard Bischoffsheim; Tel: 93 00 30 11) was designed by Charles Garnier and Gustave Eiffel. It can be toured the second and fourth Saturdays of each month at 3pm—with prior appointment.

On this relatively quiet road we can comfortably turn our attention to the splendid landscape. Shortly before the **Col des 4-Chemins** we come upon the entrance to the Paillon Valley, which give us an open view to the Alps. **La Ferme St Michel** offers a complete menu for 320FF in a delightful atmosphere; it includes everything from the aperitif to the digestif. At the same level as the Hôtel Hermitage is Le Plateau de la Justice, which is a lovely place to take a picnic. From the **Col d'Eze** (top of the pass: 1,665ft/508m) there is a

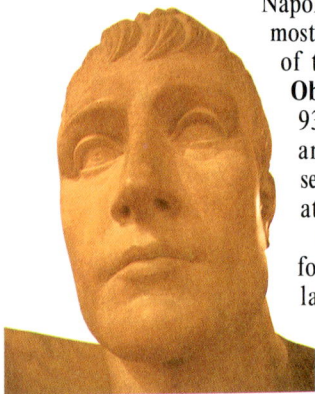

Idyllic seclusion

path which leads into the **Parc de la Revere**, in which you can study Mediterranean vegetation. From the top of the pass a splendid view opens up to the high valleys of Vésubie and Var.

The **Trophée des Alpes (Alpine Trophy)** is a restored Roman victory monument—visible from a considerable distance—in which an ornithological station has been established (Those interested in birds of prey should note that there is a trainer maintained here and it is possible to observe flight demonstrations by these winged predators). It also gave the nearby settlement its name: Tropea Augusti became **La Turbie**. The **Rue Comte de Cessole**, formerly the road to Gaul, passes by mediaeval houses to the monument, beside which there is an inviting little museum. Although mentioned in the poetry of Dante and honoured by the night time presence of Napoleon, the town radiates a pleasantly unprepossessing charm.

Roquebrune is France's only preserved permanent settlement dating from the Carolingian period (the Frankish dynasty of Charlemagne). The name of the tangled little village comes from the reddish-brown cliffs into which it was built. You should see the village on foot, in the process climbing up to the tower—the 13th-century **Donjon**, which served both for defence and as a residence. Its interior bears witness to the modest living conditions of the feudal lord.

For 500 years a procession has been taking place on the afternoon of 5 August to commemorate the one the locals held in 1467 which is said to have prevented an epidemic of the plague. Today the streets are decorated festively and illuminated with thousands of flickering oil lanterns. In the **Rue de la Fontaine**, a short way past the end of the village, there is a 1,000-year-old olive tree, believed to be the oldest in the world.

Renoir and His Olive Groves

Loafing about the harbour of St Laurent; a wealth of fauna and flora in La Gaude; Haut-de-Cagnes and the Cagne Fortress (14 miles/22km; half a day).

We depart Nice toward Cannes on the Promenade des Anglais, which turns into the six-lane coastal road.

Until 1860, when the Duchy of Nice fell to France, the **Var River** represented the border with the Kingdom of Sardinia. The town of St Laurent du Var was in charge of the river crossing. Travellers from Paris or Nice, who had to spend 12 uncomfortable days in their coaches, were carried on the shoulders of two powerful men over the ford of the torrential mountain river. How much easier it is today! It is simplicity itself to cross over the Var on the six-lane coastal highway which has been built over the now somewhat tamer river.

The imposing shopping centre, **Cap 3000**, has countless attractive boutiques and is located on the sea just beyond the airport. Here even fans of St Laurent or Jourdan can pick up bargains in the sales. The Nouvelles Galeries supermarket makes it clear just how elegant an installation of this scale can be.

St Laurent **harbour** is a nice place to take a stroll. If you feel hungry as a result of your seaside perambulations, you can dine excellently in the **Santana**. If you want to flee the hubbub of the

Gréolières-les Neiges

MONTAGNE

Cime du Cheiron 1777

DU CHEIRON

Bouyon

St. Martin-du- Var

St. Blaise

Contes

Bézaudun-les- Alpes

Le Broc

Châteauneufe-de- Contes

Castagniers

Gréolières

Var

Coursegoules

Mouton d'Anou 1085

Carros

Aspremont

Tourette-Levens

Loup

Cipières

St. Barnabé

Gattières

Colomars

Mount Chauve 854

Cantaron

Falicon

Col de Vence

St. Jeannet

St. Roman

L'Ecre

Courmes

Vence

La Gaude

Nice

Gourdon

Tourette-sur- Loup

La Barenne

Le Bar-sur- Loup

Loup

St.Paul

Le Colle-sur- Loup

St.Laurent-du- Var

Plage de la Ville

Ferry to Bastia

Magagnosc

Rouret

Cagnes

Roquefort-les- Pins

Les Maillans

Grasse

Châteauneuf-Grasse

Airport Nice- Côte d'Azur

Plascassier

Valbonne

Biot

St.Cassien-des Bois

Mouans-Sartoux

Air France

Villeneuve-Loubet- Plage

CÔTE D'AZUR

Roquette-sur- Siagne

Mougins

Zoo marin

Ferry

Pegomas

St.Jean

Vallauris

to Ajaccio, Propriano, Calvi, Ile Rousse

Le Fénerie

Le Cannet

Antibes

Cannes

Golfe-Juan

Juan- les- pins

La Bocca

Mandelieu

Golfe Juan

Cap d'Antibes

Golfe de Napoule

Ile St.Marguerite

Maure-Viell

La Napoule- Plage

Théole- sur- Mer

Ile St.Honorat

Mediterranean

La Galère

ILES DE LÉRINS

Miramar

Sea

CORNICHE

DE

L'ESTEREL

CÔTE D'AZUR

Cannes to Nice

12 km / 8 miles

Looking west from Nice

coast, a good evasive move is to take the **Corniche du Var**. This road, which provides beautiful views of the hinterlands of Nice, leads past the IBM Research Centre to **La Gaude**, where Marcel Pagnol customarily meditated. Those among us interested in fauna and flora will find a genuine 'living museum' in this former wine makers' village. **La Coupole** (Quartier St Appolouie; open from 2–6pm except Monday) was founded by the Danish sculptor Ib Schmedes, who has lived in La Gaude for 40 years.

Now, you are confronted with a pleasant choice. Starting out from La Gaude you can either drive to **St Jeannet**, passing a 14th-century castle along the way (originally owned by the Knights Templar and today—after years of renovation—occupied by the French actress, Viviane Romance) and then drive on to Vence, or you can turn back to the coast.

If you have decided in favour of the latter alternative, the monotonous residential areas of **Cagnes de Mer** turn up suddenly in the middle of the rolling landscape of the **Haut-des-Cagnes**,

which is well worth a side-trip. The best places to park are either inside the underground garage built into the mountain (an expensive but exceptionally 'landscape-friendly' solution) or up above on the castle plaza. Leaving your car, you can go by foot to discover the old city with its attractive houses, plazas, alleyways and arched passages.

In 1309 the Comte de Provence relinquished the **Cagna Fortress** to the Prince of Monaco and French Admiral Rainier Grimaldi. One year later Grimaldi had a citadel built there as a symbol of his powerful family. The *Cagnois* who sheltered within its walls cultivated wheat, wine and olives on the neighbouring hills. These staples, as well as fish from the harbour of Cros de Cagnes, were brought up into the village on mules. In the 17th century Heinrich Grimaldi had the citadel remodelled into a magnificently appointed castle. With the coming of the French Revolution this feudal life came to an abrupt end. Gaspard Grimaldi was forced to leave Cagnes and his castle along with it. He fled to Nice, a duchy which in those days still belonged to the counts of Savoy.

St Peter's Church, located beneath the Porte de Nice, is

Haut-de-Cagnes

Musée d'Art Moderne Méditerranéen

equipped with an attractive wrought-iron bell tower of the sort commonly seen in Provence. The tombs of the Grimaldis of Cagnes are also located in this church.

The Château remained unoccupied until a buyer was finally found in the 19th century. The castle has belonged to the city since 1938. Today the **Château Musée** houses the **Musée de l'Olivier Ethnographie**, in in which you can learn everything there is to know about the olive; the **Musée d'Art Moderne Méditerranéen** and the **Susy Solidor Foundation**. The latter is especially interesting—some 40 significant 20th-century artists have tried their hand at Susy's portrait. Haut-de-Cagnes has always been of great significance for modern painting. A number of German artists worked here in the 1930s. Since 1969, the castle has been host to the **Festival International de la Peinture** (30 June–30 September). For a more complete list of Côte d'Azur festivals and events, please consult the *Calendar of Special Events* on pages 108–9.

Pierre August Renoir (1841–1919) is without doubt *the* painter of Cagnes. Towards the end of the last century, suffering from gout, the artist came to the South of France on the advice of his doctor. In Cagnes he found what he sought: a hilly, idyllic landscape, a favourable microclimate and light of a special quality. It was always light which fascinated Renoir, and with his friends, Monet and Sisley, he worked in the open air, concentrating on the problems of rendering sunlight, and its reflections, on canvas.

In 1903 he established himself in the Maison de la Poste—today the city hall. In 1907 he acquired—at the advice of his friend who later became mayor of Cagnes—Les Collettes, a sizeable parcel of land with 140 old olive trees. Here he built the house in which he spent the last 12 years of his life.

In 1960 the city of Cagnes purchased the villa and installed the

Renoir's studio

Renoir Museum. Since everything was left in its original condition, the visitor feels transported back to the time when Renoir, in great pain, had to be lifted out of his bed into his wheelchair and pushed out into the garden. There he spent hours and days before the easel in the shade of his beloved olive trees.

You can dine very well in **Les Peintres** (Tel: 93 20 83 08; 71 Moutée de la Bourgarde), almost the only address where you can sample the delectable crayfish. **Josey Joe** (Tel: 93 20 68 76) is equally to be recommended. There the staff will not only give you a lecture on the different kinds of figs, but they can also conjure up a delightfully tender piece of liver. From Cagnes it is only a short distance to Vence.

Vence

Place du Peyra, the Forum of the old Roman city; the old quarter and the Cathedral; Provençal cuisine in the Auberge des Seigneurs; a treasure trove at the base of the Cathedral (from Nice 14 miles/22km; Antibes 12 miles/19km; Cannes 25 miles/39km; half a day).

Typically Provençal: Vence

Vence is only 6 miles (10km) away from the sea, and yet you get the feeling here that you are in a completely different world. The locals proudly boast: "Provence begins in Vence", and Mistral, the famous poet of this region, amplifies: *"Desempiei Arle jusquá Venco—Escoutas me Gént de Prouvenco,"* or, From Arles to Vence the people speak Provençal.

Those who have seen Chagall's painting *The Lovers of Vence* will be shocked at first, since the modern Vence outside the city walls with its horrible new buildings in no way resembles the *village perché* in the work of this poetic artist (for many centuries the farmers erected such settlements like eagles' nests at daring heights and put up fortification walls for security). However, the picturesque old Vence at the feet of the Basous—which protect it from the cold north winds—has remained unchanged, having preserved its typically Provençal character especially well.

The mediaeval core of the city, surrounded by an elliptical wall with five gates, makes it rather difficult for the visitor to imagine the Roman city of Vintium. In those days Vence was already a popular health-resort because of its mild climate, and the water from the **Source de la Foux** was just as popular for its health benefits then as now.

Coming through the Porte Peyra you come to the **Place du Peyra**, the Forum of the old Roman city. The beautiful urn-shaped fountain here dates from 1822. Passing through the **Rue du Marché**—a colourful, narrow market street with butcher, fish, cheese, vegetable, fruit, and noodle sellers—we come to the **Place Clemenceau** on our left-hand side. The City Hall is located there on the site of the former bishop's palace. In 374, shortly after Christianisation by the monks of St Honorat, Vence became an episcopal city. The Bishops Veranus (5th century) and Lambrecht (12th century) were declared saints; Farnese (16th century) declined the Vence bishop's crozier, going instead to the Holy See to become Pope Paul III. He proved to be quite generous towards Vence, donating several reliquaries, however.

Bishop Godeau (17th century) was an enthusiastic visitor of L'Hôtel des Rambouillet, then a centre of literary life, and founded the Académie Française with Richelieu. Bishop Surian (18th century) parted with his fortune for the benefit of a hospital. Vence's loss of rank as a bishop's see in 1801 can be traced to Napoleon and the Pope. At first the honour passed to Fréjus, then to the Diocese of Nice in 1860 when the left shore of the Var became permanently French.

On the site of the **Cathedral** there once stood a temple to Mars, followed by a Merovingian church. As a result of the repeated alteration and expansion of the original Roman building, the present structure is a peculiar mixture of styles. In the interior are the tombs of Saints Lambrecht and Veranus, a mosaic by Chagall in the baptismal chapel, and a choir pew of oak and pear-tree wood which was designed by J Bellot of Grasse in the 15th century; evidently—despite the five years of work which went into it—he did not lose his sense of humour.

On the Place Godeau, with the Roman Mars columns in its centre, you have a good view of the rectangular tower, a Renaissance door from 1575, courtyards and alleyways as well as a picturesque corner by the name of L'Enfer (Hell). Continuing through the **Rue St Lambert** and the **Rue de**

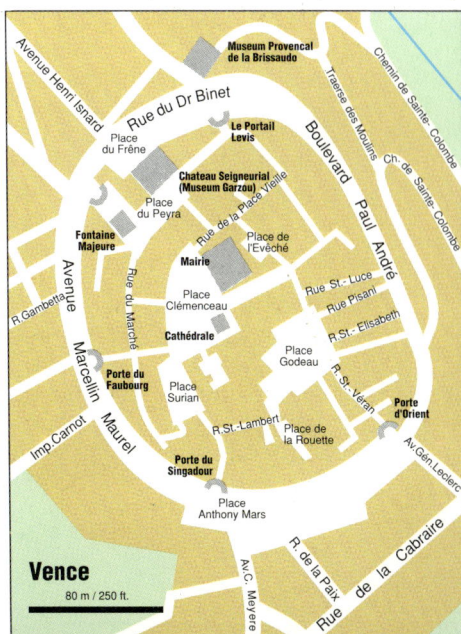

Vence

80 m / 250 ft.

l'Hotel de Ville you come to the **Porte du Singadour**. Directly opposite it is a 15th-century fountain. If you turn off to the left you pass by the **Port de l'Orient**, for which you once needed to have your own key. The date up on the left commemorates the unsuccessful siege of the city by the Huguenots. The old Alphonse Toreille Seminary, constructed by Godeau in 1669, is located a short distance from here. The **Boulevard Paul André** leads along the city wall, large sections of which are still preserved. The view of the Baous and the outer spurs of the Alps is beautiful here.

Now we return to the **Place du Peyra** by way of the **Portail Lévis** and the **Rue du Portail Lévis**. The castle erected by Villenueve in the 16th century is located on the **Place Thiers**. Today it houses the **Museum Carzou**. The painter Carzou, who has small ironic blue eyes, a high forehead and white hair, bought an old *mas* (a southern French farmhouse) in Vence in 1958, because here he could find the quiet, the relaxation and the freedom of spirit necessary for his creativity.

The paintings, watercolours, drawings, sculpture and books exhibited in the castle were donated to the museum by Carzou. At the moment he is working on the design of a chapel in Manousque. The old **ash tree** on the plaza in front of the château is supposed to have been planted in the 16th century, in honour of Franz I and Pope Paul III. The restaurant **Auberge des Deigneurs** serves Provençal dishes in a dining room with a large, beautiful fireplace. According to rumour, the restaurant is supposed to have lost its star because representatives from the Michelin guides were served a dessert in the shape of a penis.

Many artists were attracted to Vence after the First World War. Among others, André Gide, Paul Valéry, Chaim Soutine and Raoul Dufy made extended visits. In 1955, when the city had no more than 6,000 inhabitants, a new generation of artists came to Vence: Céline, Tzara, and Cocteau; Matisse, Chagall, Carzou and

Spoiled for choice

Dubuffet. Today Vence has a population of 15,000, and its artistic tradition continues.

Arman, born in Nice, has been an American citizen since 1972, but every year he leaves New York to work and celebrate in Vence. His house, which originally looked like an overturned, half-buried boat, now rather resembles a work of art. The wing added in 1980 is ornamented with 2,300 wash-tubs.

The artist Nall has established himself in Dubuffet's former studio. Dali, of whom he thought very highly, is supposed to have said to him: "If you can succeed in portraying hair in such a way that you are convinced you can see it growing, then you can really paint." It is true that Nall observes nature, but he doesn't copy it. It is also worthy of note that he gives young alcoholics and drug addicts painting lessons.

At the base of the Cathedral, Georges Martin has a business which is frequently closed, since he has been working alone for 30 years. If you are looking for old wooden doors, closets, communion tables, window bars, fireplace grilles or wrought iron gates, then you should arrange a visit to this exquisite trove of finds by telephone (Tel: 93 58 11 47).

Vence is not just an attractive vacation town, it's also a good starting point for excursions into the splendid hinterlands. I am pleased to provide lodging in my restored farm to individualists, art fans or those in need of relaxation who would like to get to know a bit of the real near-coastal Provence (by previous arrangement only; 659 Chemin de la Gaude; Tel: 93 58 74 87). The first time you call you'll be picked up, since the route is complicated to describe.

You can enjoy very good Provençal cuisine in the **Farigoule** (Tel: 93 58 01 27) at 15 Rue Jean Isnard. The proprietress is some-times quite severe; you should definitely make reservations. You can also sit outside in the **Closerie des Genéts**. The food is very good, although the service can leave something to be desired.

A VENCE, VISITEZ LE CHATEAU-MUSEE
NOTRE DAME DES FLEURS
Musée du parfum et de la liqueur

Ancienne demeure des Evêques de Vence classée monument historique. 900 m² d'exposition dont : salles médiévales et cellules monacales du XIe s. Chapelle romane décorée d'icônes et de vitraux d'art, abritant une sculpture de la Vierge du VIe s. Collection de tapisseries peintes à la main évoquant l'histoire de la Haute Epoque. 40 machines anciennes retraçant l'histoire de la fabrication des parfums et des liqueurs.
Jardins de plantes à parfums dominant le littoral du Cap Ferrat à l'Estérel (cf. Guide Michelin). Enfin pour tous les gourmets, dans la salle capitulaire de l'ancienne abbaye, un restaurant gastronomique vous fera découvrir la cuisine des arômes. A la sortie du musée, vente de produits régionaux fabriqués sur place et dégustation gratuite de liqueurs.

A LA SORTIE DE VENCE : PRENDRE LA DIRECTION TOURRETTES-GRASSE SUR 2,5 KM
CHATEAU NOTRE DAME DES FLEURS · 2635, ROUTE DE GRASSE · 06140 VENCE · 93 58 06 00

Heures d'ouverture
été : 10 h-12 h 30 - 14 h-18 h 30
hiver : 10 h-12 h 30 - 14 h-17 h 30
Fermé le dimanche matin

Entrée : 12 F
Groupes, étudiants, enfants, 3e âge, et aux possesseurs de cette carte : 7 F
Gratuité pour les moins de 12 ans

AROUND VENCE

Peaceful Mountain Villages

The Chapelle du Rosaire by Matisse; on the summits of the Baous; gormandizing in the Auberge de St Jeannet; the mountain village of Gattières; the idyllic village of Le Broc; a snack at a ranch (about half a day, 38 miles/60km).

Vence viaduct

We leave Vence heading north on the D2210, but we have to watch carefully to avoid driving past the Provençal building with a gilded cross on its glazed tiled roof. Matisse was 80 years old when he designed and decorated the **Chapelle du Rosaire** (1947–51). It's certainly worth a tour, although this is only possible on Tuesdays and Thursdays (information from the Syndicat d'Initiative Vence. Tel: 93 58 06 38).

Continuing our drive we can already make out the imposing south face of the **Baou de St Jeannet**. However, this shouldn't keep us from pulling over into the first lay-by and taking a view of the fully intact city wall surrounding Vence. In doing so we also discover a **viaduct**, a vestige of the 'good old days' when you could still ride on the single track railway from Nice to Draguignon. The tunnels for this train line, destroyed by the Germans during World War II, serve today for the cultivation of especially tasty mushrooms. Up to now, this gastronomically important fact has prevented the train from being put back into service as a tourist attraction.

A short way before we turn from the roundabout onto the cul-de-sac that leads up to St Jeannet, the souvenir hunters among us have a chance to purchase bizarrely formed hollowed-out gourds, some of which are also hand-painted by the daughter of the flourishing family enterprise found there.

St Jeannet is a popular destination for mountain climbers with experience on sheer rock-faces. The **Baou**, towering 1,300ft (400m)

60

St Jeannet

over the village, has some 35 different possible ascents; if you have suitable shoes you can also reach the summit—from which there is a splendid panorama—comfortably in about an hour's hike.

The 'initiates' who seek out the **Auberge de St Jeannet** can enjoy—accompanied by a bottle of wine from the small local vineyard—the specialities which Antoine enthusiastically prepares for his guests: cold smoked breast of duck served on fresh baby leaf spinach glazed with hazelnut oil, ravioli filled with *loup-farce* in a basil sauce, duck filet with a hint of wild mountain honey, or *carré d'agneau* (lamb) in a mild garlic sauce. The walls are hung with the works of contemporary artists (among whom I count myself), which are available for sale.

On the other hand, the beautiful view down to the coast is free of charge. It has provided an inspiration for such painters as Dunoyer de Segonzac, Carzou, Chagall and Poussin. On a tour through the village, say to the chapel on the other end, you might run into the old Colonel hobbling along on crutches, conscientiously performing the duty to which he has been appointed: delivering telegrams and express mail.

Our next destination is the village of **Gattières**. It goes without saying that fans of picturesque alleyways are in the right place here. The view of the Alps is especially impressive. Winter sports fans can pursue their passion on the 75 miles (120km) of ski trails at **Isola 2000** (elevation 9,800ft/3,000m)—only 75mins from Nice.

The D2209 is the main road above the Var River (unfortunately rather tamed these days) through the border region of the pre-Alps from **Grasse** to **Carros**. The latter's attractive houses are marshalled around a castle; a little below them, next to an old mill, there is an observation platform with a panoramic view. The 'new' Carros

Carros

may be the pride of the community, but it disfigures the area with its obtrusive new buildings. From here on the villages become smaller, quieter and more untouched.

Le Broc (*broco* means olive-cutting) was quite popular with a number of bishops who sought relaxation here. This splendidly located village possesses an idyllic plaza with arcaded buildings. There is also a fountain whose cool waters have saved more than a few hikers, coming over the mountain from St Jeannet, from heat exhaustion—including me! You can best tame your growling stomach at **Chez Guy**: the pizza, topped with strictly fresh ingredients, is reasonably priced and has a flavour delightfully suggestive of a wild mountain landscape.

Bouyon, once a border village between Nice and Savoy, has only 229 residents. These are mostly senior citizens, since the younger people have left in search of employment. It's probably for this reason that so many houses are for sale around the rectangular village plaza. Speculators will almost certainly be rewarded for their risk in a few years. The view is fantastic over the Cheiron, the Var and Esteron Valleys and the Alps of the French-Italian border region.

Now we take the D8 through an ever more wild and deserted region along the Le Chiers mountain-range, thus arriving at **Bezaudun-les-Alpes**, where fanciers of old doors could be induced to commit criminal deeds. Above the gorge of Cagne River the tall façades of the houses of **Coursegoules** seem to reach for the sky. If lady luck is smiling on you and the door of the church is unlocked, you should pass a couple of minutes admiring the panels painted by the omnipresent Louis Bréa.

High above the Cagne River, which swells during the rainy season and can then boast some beautiful waterfalls, we drive back to Vence: on the left, the **Ranch El Bronco** (Tel: 93 58 09 83) offers horse riders the chance to take a lovely excursion—with guide—through a charming but spartan thyme-scented landscape.

Afterwards, for the saddle-sore, weary and hungry, a meal at the simple tables of the ranch (the salad features an outstandingly good olive oil) tastes especially fine. (Those interested in riding elsewher on the Côte d'Azur will want to consult the *What to Know* section for 'Sport', pages 115–117, where stables are listed in 11 areas).

Just past the **Col de Vence** (pass altitude 3,700ft/1,128m) drive as slowly as possible—the view is unique. From here you can survey the whole mountain chain between the left bank of the Var and Mont Agel, the coast with Cap Ferrat, the Baie des Anges of Nice, the Antibes Peninsula, the Isle St Marguerite near Cannes and the Esterel Massif. The local amateur bicycle racers—you can't wish them away—will appreciate your moderate speed. In gleaming outfits they careen down the mountain—mostly in groups—towards Vence. When you imagine the effort it must have taken to pedal up to the top of the pass, you won't mind in the least making way for their hair-raising downhill race.

St Paul → Canne.

ST Paul

St Paul—an artists' colony with tradition; handicrafts in the Rue Grande; dining in the renowned Colombe d'Or; the Fondation Maeght, a lively museum of modern art; back to the coast; the horse-racing track Hippodrom de la Côte d'Azur (Nice 12 miles/20km, Vence 3 miles/4.5km; half a day).

Gently rolling hills and fertile valleys (which have unfortunately become densely settled) surround the silhouette of **St Paul de Vence**, a village originally built as a border fortification in the 16th century. In the 1920s it was 'discovered' by painters like Signac, Bonnard, Modigliani and Soutine.

These young, as yet unknown artists lodged in the modest *auberge* at the village entrance, where they were able to pay with their paintings—a fact which got around quickly. Derain, Utrillo,

Vlaminck and Matisse came, followed by such young intellectuals as Prévert, Camus, Giono, Maeterlinck, Morand and Kipling, who transformed the village into a sort of 'Saint-Germain-des-Prés-de-la-mer'. Finally, in the 1940s film people joined the party. Today it is rather difficult to imagine the peace and quiet of this once so typical Provençal village. Since then St Paul has become one of the most popular tourist destinations in France. The modest lodge has turned into a pompous hotel, and only those who stroll through dimly illuminated alleyways by night can get an idea of the village's earlier charm.

The **Rue Grande**—the narrow, cobble-stoned main street—cuts through the length of the village. In the almost *too* beautifully re-stored old houses, decorated with their coats of arms, there are shops and galleries for arts and handicrafts. You should get up early in the morning if you want to enjoy the atmosphere here undisturbed by the tangle of languages of your fellow humans as they pile out of their coaches later in the day. You will be glad you made the effort as you take in the little plaza with the urn-shaped fountain and the vaulted washing-house; glimpse inside a church; spend a couple of minutes at Chagall's grave and make your way back along the village wall to the **Café de la Place**, where you can get an especially good *café crème* and skim the pages of the *Nice Matin* (the local newspaper). Along the way you will also encounter the friendly and expressive faces of the local farmers and flower growers. You might also see the men playing *boule*—a passionate dedication for many of them—among them, perhaps, the old man who uses a magnet to help him pick up the heavy iron ball (since he cannot bend over so well anymore) or the 'young father', Montand, who has remained true to 'his village'.

Many of those whose images still linger in my mind's eye are no longer there: Lino Ventura, James Baldwin, Chagall, Kurt Jürgens . . . and the old white-haired lady who radiated so much dignity with her beautiful peasant face—her portrait hangs in the bar of the famed **Colombe d'Or**. She used to sit right there—La Mère Roux—in her plain black dress. It was not her cane, rather simply

The festive interior of the Colombe d'Or

her *presence* which motivated the waiters to do their job even more nimbly and attentively. A drink under these arches—and in between a walk through the dining room with its painted wooden ceiling and works by Picasso, Dufy, Léger, Calder, Chagall and Matisse—harmonises just as well with lunch as it does with evenings on the beautiful terrace (as long as you've reserved a table in time). It is this unique ambience which makes this restaurant one of the most beautiful in the world. The *hors d'oeuvres* are recommended, even though you always nibble too many of them—something that goes unnoticed, of course, until the main course is served. You should try the tender, rose-hued *lamb carré* and for dessert a *soufflé Grand Marnier*, which always disappears faster than its (air-puffed) size would lead you to believe.

A visit to the **Fondation Maeght** is an experience which even art-haters shouldn't pass up. We owe a debt to the art-dealer couple Aimé and Marguerite Maeght for this most beautiful and lively museum of modern art. They created this complex with the help of Spanish architect José Luis Sert. The two main buildings of the museum constructed of a light coloured concrete and red brick, are adorned by a basin-like roof design reminiscent of a Mediterranean rain storage tank. In addition to the museum's considerable collection there are significant exhibitions each year based on a particular theme or the work of a contemporary painter. Between the buildings is the **Giacometti-Ho**, a splendid park with a gigantic sculpture by Calder, a variety of mobiles, a fountain with moving metal cylinders, and other sculptures and ceramics (mornings from 10am–12.30pm and 3–7pm afternoons; located ⅔ of a mile [1km] north-west of St Paul de Vence (D7).

Leaving the Fondation we drive via the **Colle sur Loup** (numerous antique shops on the main street) back to Capres-sur-Mer. Our excursion into the past comes to an abrupt end at the coast. If you

Fondation Maeght

depart Cagnes in the direction of Antibes, on your right is a beautiful horse-racing track, the **Hippodrom de la Côte d'Azur**. Betting fans can try their luck there for as little as five francs (mid-December–mid-March and 30 June–1 Sept). One person's misfortune is sometimes another's gain: I owe my house to a passion for gambling—not mine, but that of its previous owner.

A bit further on the pyramid-shaped apartment complex **Marina Baie des Anges** pops up—you can't miss it. Its modern architecture inflames tempers over and over again. From their plant-hung terraces the owners of the penthouse-like condominiums can keep an eye on their boats, which are moored in the 'most beautiful yacht-harbour in the world' as is modestly proclaimed at the entrance of the residential complex.

Villeneuve-Loubet and Escoffier

The medieval Château Villeneuve and the Musée d'Art Culinaire (only open in the afternoons); the Siesta: restaurant, gambling casino and disco in one; Marineland (Nice 10 miles/16km; Cannes 14 miles/23km; Antibes 7½ miles/12km; Vence 7½ miles/12km).

Villeneuve-Loubet is located inland. The medieval Château Villeneuve which rises above the old core of the city is where the Peace Treaty of Nice was signed in 1538.

It is by no means a displeasure to me that one of my cookery books is displayed in the **Musée d'Art Culinaire** (behind the *Mairie* or town hall). The Auguste Escoffier Foundation was founded in 1966 with the aim of creating a museum of culinary arts in the house in which 'the king of chefs and the chef of kings' was born—in recognition of the services which he, with his talent and creations, rendered to the world of cuisine.

The most important meeting of his life was with César Ritz, for whom he first worked in 1883 in the Grand Hotel in Monte

67

Carlo. When Ritz took over the Savoy in London, this became—thanks not least to Escoffier—the meeting place for the international 'jet-set' of that era. In 1898 Ritz opened, in Paris, the establishment which bears his name. Again it was Escoffier to whom the hotel owed its immediate success. In 1899 he followed Ritz into London's Carlton, which he did not leave until 1920, when he finally returned to Monte Carlo at 74 years of age; he died on 12 February 1935. A less well-known fact is that Escoffier developed the *bouillon* cube together with Julius Maggi.

Léo Isba is another man who is equally connected with Villeneuve-Loubet. In 1948 he designed his first handbag, which he named 'New Look'. On the occasion of the 1972 Olympics he equipped

Musée de l'Art Culinaire

the French delegation with bags. Today in his Villeneuve-Loubet factory he designs not only handbags, but also belts, leather clothing and jewellery. His trademark golden palm on a black background has now become synonymous with fine accessories.

On the beach next to where the **Loup** flows rather unobtrusively into the sea you will find the **Siesta**, an open-air night club with casino, a restaurant and seven dance floors. The admission to such establishments in France is not cheap. It can be expensive if you want to be where the action is, and entrance and your first drink here will cost you in the region of 130FF.

Marineland, a sort of aquatic zoo, familiar to American visitors who have been to the Californian prototype, beckons from the other side of the railway tracks. Parents with children will surely not be allowed to sneak past it.

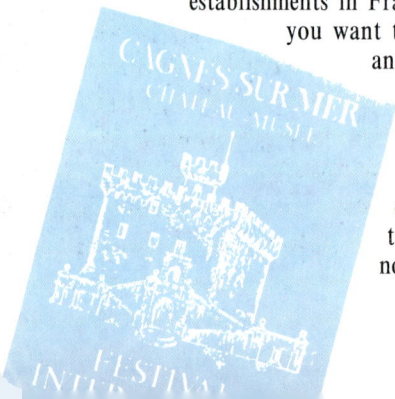

Valbonne: Another Silicon Valley

The old and new side by side: A village with a history extending back to antiquity and the Sophia Antipolis high-technology center; a broad variety of recreational opportunities. (Cannes 8 miles/13km, Antibes 10½ miles/17km, Mougin 4 miles/6.5km, Nice 18½ miles/30km.)

'Vallis bona' (the Happy Valley) has been cultivated since antiquity. The history of **Valbonne** extends back to the founding of the monastery of the Chalais Order in the 13th century. The **parish church**, on the shore of the river below the village, belonged to the former abbey. The village centre is the **Place des Arcades** in the shadows of old elm-trees. The pretty old fountain is worth a look.

Valbonne owes its modern-day importance to Pierre Lafitte, the former director of the highly respected Paris School of Engineering. He created the 'clean' International High-Tech-Centre located on a plateau to the south-east of Valbonne following the American example of Silicon Valley. It has a convenient location for transport, not far from the Nice International Airport and the Autoroute A8. Its sport installations—swimming pools, golf, playing fields—art and cultural projects can offer its highly qualified scientists a broad range of recreational opportunities. More than 150 domestic and foreign companies and institutes have already established themselves here.

"One day this region will be considered the California of Europe," proclaimed founder Lafitte, a native of St Paul de Vence. The success to date seems to be proving him right.

Kitsch to Kitchenware

Antibes

Artists and Shipbuilders

The Château Grimaldi and its exhibitions; the Musée Picasso; the Romanesque Cathedral; the old market-hall on the Cours Masséna; Plage de la Gravette; Port Vauban Yacht Harbour; fine dining in the Restaurant Regal (Cannes 7 miles/11km, Nice 14 miles/22km; half a day).

"I paint Antibes, a small fortified city. Entirely in the gleam of the sun, it rises up from the beautiful mountains and the eternally snow-covered ranges of the Alps. One ought to paint it with gold and precious gems." These are the enthusiastic words of Claude Monet, who resided in **Antibes** in 1888. In contrast to Picasso's paintings, which he left to the city only under the condition that they could never be lent out, the 36 paintings Monet produced here are now in the USA.

The Greek city of Antipolis (Antibes) was founded at the same time as Nikaia (Nice). From 1386 on, the city belonged to the Grimaldis, falling into the possession of Henry IV at the end of the 14th century. Since the King recognised its strategic significance he made it into a border fortification which was finally completed by Vauban. Today the **Fort Carré** is all that is left of Vauban's work. The view from the fortified walls is spectacular—did Napoleon know to treasure it when he was held as a prisoner in Fort Carré after the fall of Robespierre? Or did the interned painters and writers who fled from Hitler to the Côte?

The Château Grimaldi was laid out in the 12th century, following the design of an ancient Roman fort. The rectangular tower, battlements and several window openings are all that remain from

70

that period. The rest of the complex was reconstructed in the 16th century. Arman's predilection for stringed instruments is admirably documented in the interior courtyard. The earliest known illustration of the City of Antibes is in the background of a 1539 painting by Aundi in the chapel. There are works by Germaine Richier, César, Miró, Pagés and Armado on the garden terrace, which faces the sea. The main attraction, however, is the **Musée Picasso**, which is housed in the castle. In it you get a sense of what Picasso must have felt during his stay here in 1946: *joie de vivre* and serenity. This happiness didn't come from out of the blue—the war was finally over, there was the splendid studio, provided by the director of the local museum, the sun and light of the South, a new 'young' love (Françoise Gilot, whose book I recommend), renewed father-hood and good friends such as Prévert and Eluard.

In addition to Picasso's work the museum possesses a collection of contemporary works by Léger, Magnelli, Hartung and Max Ernst as well as the Russian-French painter Nicolas de Staël. The latter lived in Antibes for some time and is said to have plunged to his death from his terrace in 1955.

If you're interested in history you can examine finds from Antibes and the surrounding area (from both water and land) in

Still life in Antibes harbour

the **Musée Archéologique**, which is housed in the Bastion St André constructed by Vauban. The Romanesque **Cathedral** is located right next to the fortress.

The **Cours Masséna** is filled with delightful scents of the Provence—in the old market hall everything to please the heart and the senses is bought and sold in an animated and cheerful at-mosphere. Only a few steps away, on the **Place Odibert**, there is a flea market on Thursday and Saturday. The **Musée Peynet**, located on the **Place Nationale**, has drawings which are known virtually

Isolated beach in Antibes

the world over. You can relax at a café or restaurant terrace under the shade of the plane trees and, with a bit of luck, you might hear a melody floating out of a window played by Sidney Bichet, the renowned composer and trumpet player.

If you want to take a refreshing dip in the sea, the **Plage de la Gravette** is a sheltered bay with a beach of the finest sand. Below the market hall there is an **English Pub** where you can quench your thirst with a freshly tapped beer. In the evenings it's hard to find a seat, but it's a good place to make new acquaintances. French is hardly spoken there. The customers talk a lot about boats—and girls.

Antibes has four yacht harbours with almost 3,000 berths. The most magnificent luxury yachts set anchor in the modern **Port Vauban Yacht Harbour**, located near the harbour offices. The boats look like something out of *1001 Nights*—which is also the name of the quay on which they're docked. George Nicholson, one of the best-known shipbuilders, knows the yachts, their owners, and their histories. He will tell you that Adnan Kashoggi, for example, owner of the *Nabila*, really loved the sea and spent six months a year on his yacht. Countless gossip columnists made a living from reporting his parties.

Donald Trump bought the *Nabila* and renamed it *Princess Trump*. When he found out that it wasn't the largest yacht in the world, he came unhappily to Nicholson: "Could you lengthen it for me?" he wanted to know in all seriousness. The yacht has, in fact, now been lengthened! Nonetheless the *Princess Trump* is still smaller than the royal yacht *Britannia*, of the British royal family, and Stavros Niarchos's *Atlantis*, which docks in Monte Carlo harbour. The largest of all belongs to King Fahd of Saudi Arabia.

The most beautiful yacht is the *Corinthia*, berthed at Porto Canto in Cannes. People still talk about the party that the Prince de Lignac gave on his *New Horizon I* at St Tropez' Pampelonne Beach: even if the Prince isn't *really* a prince, his ship resembles a palace. The *Stalca* belongs to the royal family of Monaco and is named after St̲éphanie, A̲lbert and C̲aroline.

The wines of the **Domaines Ott** are among the most famous of the Provence. Since her divorce, Anne Ott has managed the **Mas de la Pagana**, an enchanting little hotel with country charm. It has only 10 rooms and a terrace where you can dine cheerfully and well. Henri Varaud, former head chef of the Carlton in Cannes, now pampers his guests in the **Régal**, 5 Rue du Sade. If you like spicy food you should definitely sample the *crêpe diabolique*.

Cap d'Antibes—Eldorado of Luxury

'Peninsula of the rich'; fish in the Restaurant de Bacon; panoramic view of the Alps, the popular vacation town of Juan-les-Pins; dining in the garden of the Auberge d'Esterel; Golfe Juan (tour of the peninsula roughly 6 miles/10km—allow 2 hours; with Juan les Pins and Golfe Juan allow half a day).

The entrance to Jardin Thuret

The gorgeous **Cap d'Antibes** peninsula is located between Antibes and Juan-les-Pins. The **La Salis** beach provides swimmers with a splendid panorama. A drive—or better, a walk around the peninsula (there are both smugglers' and customs agents' paths) is well worthwhile. Here and there between the parking ramps of the famous luxury hotels you can see large greenhouses, small Provençal country houses or a childrens' summer camp.

The **Restaurant de Bacon** is known for its excellent fish dishes. On the highest point of the Cap we find a splendid panorama stretching from Esterel to the Alps, a **pilgrimage church** with charming votive plaques and a **lighthouse** whose beams reach my bedroom in Vence. The **Plage de la Garoupe** is one of the most beautiful sand beaches in the region. The first eucalyptus trees, introduced from Australia, were planted in the **Jardin Thuret** around the middle of the last century. All the way out on the end of the point is the renowned **Hôtel du Cap**, whose illustrious guests of the 1920's introduced the 'summer season' to the Côte. Anthony Quinn, Lauren Bacall, Sylvester Stallone and Arnold Schwarzenegger enjoyed its luxuries during the 1990 film festival. **Musée Naval et Napoléonien** awakens memories of the French Emperor who fled here from Elba.

Juan-les-Pins is located on the other side of the peninsula in a beautiful sheltered inlet. This vacation town, especially popular among young people, is famous for its **Jazz Festival** in July, its long beach of fine sand, the attractive yacht and fishermens' harbour—and its nightlife. (Other jazz festivals, chamber music recitals and musical evenings throughout the Côte are listed in the *Calendar of Special Events* section, pages 108–109.)

Unfortunately, the old casino was demolished, so now the balls roll in an ultramodern palace of blue glass. The grove with the hundred-year-old pines which Florence Gould fell in love (see page 16) with creates the backdrop for an annual open-air festival featuring many greats of jazz music.

The two street-cafés **Pam-Pam** and **Le Festival** are open into the early morning hours. Night-owls can quench their thirst with exotic cocktails as steamy Latin American rhythms, played by a three-man-band, thunder out of oversized loudspeakers at 150 decibels. With the long business hours here, those who feel that they simply *must* down another cocktail before visiting the disco or casino won't have any problem. The delightful garden of the **Auberge d'Esterel** is a good alternative for anyone who likes things a bit quieter.

The **Golfe Juan** has a harbour for yachts and fishing-boats, a sand beach which was still almost deserted in Picasso's days (from 1926) as well as a beautiful view over to the Lérins Islands and the Cap d'Antibes. The **Tetou**—a chic pilgrimage destination for *bouillabaise* fans—is also here. You have to make reservations, and credit cards are not accepted—nevertheless this is a decidedly expensive pleasure.

The Tetou at Golfe Juan

Vallauris—Ceramics, Art and Kitsch

'The Ceramic Capital'—a romantic town on a gently rolling hill where Picasso once lived; the artist's 'War and Peace' in the Romanesque chapel (Cannes 4 miles/6km, Antibes 5 miles/8km, Nice 20 miles/31km; allow 2–3 hours).

Vallauris, just over a mile (2km) north-west of Golfe Juan, was already a potters' town in Roman times. In the 16th century this tradition was continued by Italian potters who the Bishop brought in from Grasse. Even so, without Picasso, **Vallauris** would certainly not be the 'Ceramic Capital'. From 1947–55 he lived in La Galloise, a house whose simplicity Cocteau made light of during a visit (he also didn't think much of the village's "destitute splendour"). Picasso's answer was simple: for the first two years he worked in the Madoura pottery workshop, whose owners, Susanne and Georges Ramié, he met on the beach of Golfe Juan. In 1950 he was named an honorary citizen. He took his revenge for this with the bronze sculpture *Man with Sheep*. In 1952 he created his landmark work, *War and Peace*, thus making the little Romanesque chapel (which had escaped the destruction of the original monastery) into a monu-

ment for peace. The castle, which was rebuilt in the 16th century, contains the city's museum. It houses ceramic works by Picasso and the Magnelli Foundation.

In the same year that I made my first visit to France, with my father, I also made my first visit to Picasso. I fell eternally love with both Pablo, the man and artist, and with Vallauris, a romantic little town set on gently rolling hills. My love for Picasso has remained, but not for Vallauris. Françoise Gilot, his former lifetime companion, has very clearly expressed a feeling which I share: "Pablo's presence brought the town affluence, but his example was not understood. Today Vallauris is a stronghold of bad taste." Countless ceramic workshops and stores sell huge amounts of kitsch. Today over 200 potters live in Vallauris, and since 1966 an international biennial for ceramic art has been held here. The **Galerie Madoura**, owned by the Ramiés' son, is still among the best pottery workshops in town. Besides their own creations they also produce copies of Picasso's works, which are easily confused for originals by unknowledgable tourists. Picasso left Vallauris in 1955. On the occasion of his 90th birthday the city put on a huge folk-festival—in which, however, Picasso didn't take part. He explained: "I am helpful for your spectacle, but I don't want to *be* your spectacle." He watched the festival on television. You can get good food in the **Gousse d'Ail**, 11 Avenue Grasse; Tel: 93 64 10 71.

Vallauris has a new attraction for the 1990s, and once again, there is a big name to draw the crowds: at the **Jean Marais Festival** (July/August), a prize is given to the best young actor. However, Marais, the 76-year-old actor and sculptor is wise enough not to organise the festival himself. The director is Nicolas Briançon, a former assistant to Marais who dreamed of presenting *Les Chevaliers de la Table Ronde* at the first festival. Would Marais, who now has his hands full as a sculptor— preparing a statue for the Theatre Montpensier de Versailles, a sculpture for Vallauris, and a work for Brussels—also play? The friend of Cocteau remarked: "To appear in one's own festival—isn't that embarrassing?"

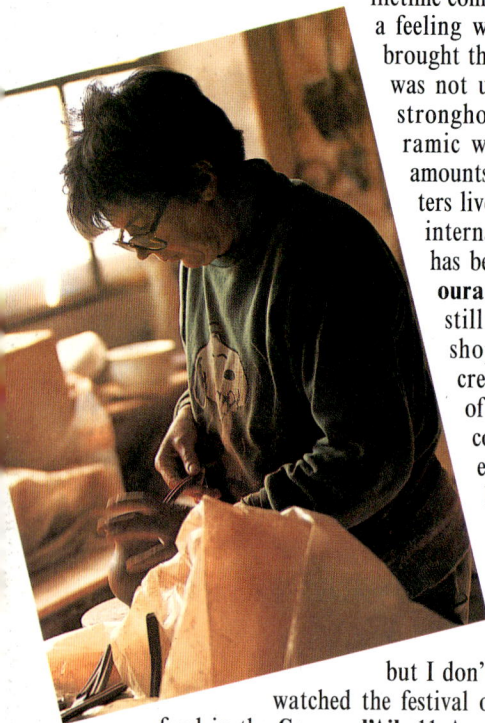

76

Cannes

Glamour and Money

Belle Epoque buildings, high society, festivals and culinary delights, the Croisette—a world-renowned shoreline promenade, the Festival-Palais, the old harbour, the main business street Rue d'Antibes, seafood at Astoux et Brun (allow an entire day).

The are only a few places in the world which call themselves 'the world'—*le monde*. Without question, Cannes is among them. It all started in 1834, when Lord Brougham discovered the little fishing village by chance. Due to a cholera epidemic, he and his ailing daughter were forced, against their will, to stay in an *auberge* in the lower Suquet. He was so pleased by the *bouillabaise* served there, the harbour, the islands, and the pines and olive groves that he never arrived in Nice—the actual destination of his journey—and instead settled in Cannes. From then on—for the next 34 years—the rich lord spent his winters in his villa, Eléonore Louise. His example started a trend which turned Portus Canuae, the Roman harbour, into a seaside resort with a world-wide reputation. By 1870 the city already had 35 hotels and 200 villas.

"Princes, princes, nothing but princes" groaned de Maupassant, who frequently sailed in the bay of La Napoule between 1884 and 1888. "If you like them you're in the right place!" In Cannes, the architects of the Belle Epoque era had the opportunity to bring their most insane dreams to realisation. Pompous villas, extravagant

palaces and dreamlike gardens appeared on the hills of La Californie, Croix-des-Gardes, Le Cannet and Super-Cannes. The **Villa Alexandra**, with its minarets, could be mistaken for a mosque; **Château Scott** is Gothic in style; the **Villa Camille Amélie** has a natural grotto and huge marble columns; the **Villa Yakimour** was built by the Aga Khan for Yvette Labrousse.

Cannes is no city of the arts, even though there is scarcely a French writer or artist who hasn't spent some time here. But it is, without doubt, an unusual place. A town of pleasures, of strolling and spending money, of yacht-mania and of festivals; an oasis for international high society, an Eldorado for gourmets, who come to be spoiled by some of the world's great chefs (Sylvain Duparc in the **Carlton**, Claude Willer in the **Martinez**, Jacques Chibois in the **Royal Gray**, Claude Verger in the **Villa Dionysos**), but also for fans of local specialities—at affordable prices.

There are over 300 restaurants awaiting you in the Avenue Félix Faure, the Forville Market, in the Suquet quarter, at the Quai St-Pierre and in the streets between the Croisette and the Rue d'Antibes. Everywhere you go there is a wonderful scent of garlic, truffles, herbs and spices. The local cuisine is, in the words of poet Stephen Liègard, *"comme une tranch de soleil sur une nappe de mer bleue"* (like a spot of sunlight on a cloth of sea-blue).

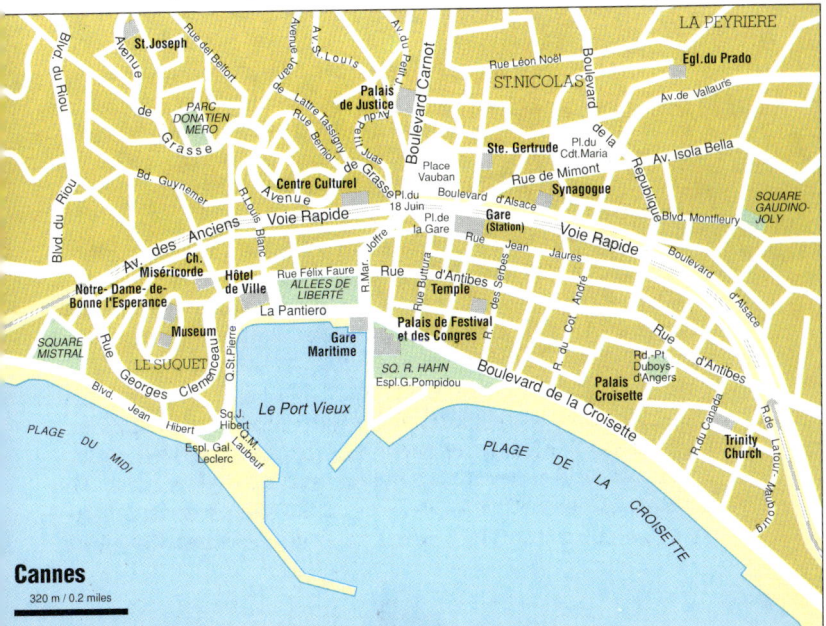

Cannes

320 m / 0.2 miles

The **Croisette**, at the beginning of the century the boulevard of kings and musicians, is quite the most international shoreline promenade in the world today—as attested by the 96 newspapers in 30 different languages that you will find on sale. This magnificent street, with its tall palm trees and colourful, relaxing gardens and parks, extends from **Palm Beach** (open only in summer) up to the **Casino Municipal**. By the way, Palm Beach was constructed in 1928, the same year as the notorious *jeudi noir*—the largest stock-market crash of all time. Palatial hotels, terrace cafés and luxury boutiques hem the city side of the four-lane boulevard; the sea beckons us with its sandy beaches and excellent fish restaurants; benches and chairs invite you to loll about for a while as the constantly smiling ice-cream vendours wheel their carts past.

The most beautiful hotel in Cannes

The notorious *monstres sacrés* (holy monsters) of the Belle Epoque, such as the Carlton, the Majestic and the Martinez, have been completely renovated. The most beautiful hotel is still the Carlton, constructed in 1913 with its *coupoles d'angle* (cupola roofs), which are said to be modelled on the perfect breasts of the beautiful Otero. The **Palais des Festivals et des Congrés** is where—among other things—the film festival takes place. It is called 'the Bunker' in the local vernacular—a modern complex of glass and concrete whose architecture has stimulated some heated debate. Nonetheless, it has the most up-to-date appointments, and in its gigantic underground garage (950 spaces) you can guarantee that your car will always be well looked after.

In the **old harbour** the fishing boats dock right alongside luxury yachts. The *Galion Neptune*, the ship used in the Roman Polanski film *Pirates,* can be toured for a few francs. It might be considered as the symbol of this film city. The **Rue d'Antibes**, which runs parallel to the Croisette, is Cannes' main business street. It is frequently compared with the Rue de Faubourg Saint-Honoré in Paris, and the prices are certainly similar. What was Cocteau's recommendation? "One can certainly leave the house without an umbrella, but never without one's wallet—the selection is simply too alluring." Opposite the festival hall are the **Allées de la Liberté**, an attractive place for a stroll, with a flower market in the

The Lêrins Islands, home of the *Son et Lumière*

mornings and a flea market on Saturdays. If you're a fan of fresh seafood, you should definitely stop by **Astoux et Brun** (right on the corner; 24, rue Felix Foure, Tel: 93 39 92 87).

The city's former main traffic artery—the **Rue Meynadier**—connects the city centre with the Suquet quarter, its oldest section. A cheese shop, noodle shop, two butchers' shops and a *traiteur* were awarded medals for the quality of their wares. The **Forville Market** is a real feast for the eyes (daily except Sundays). Here you can get not only the best fruit, the crispest vegetables and the freshest fish—you are also taking part in a spectacle which even the *Cannois* are unable to pass up. The **Rue St Antoine**, in whose low buildings a number of restaurants have been established, leads us to the **Place de la Castre**, from which we can enjoy a very beautiful view. **Old Cannes** around the Suquet Hills consists only of seven or eight narrow streets, each one more beautiful than the last. The rectangular 72ft (22m) tall **Soquet Tower** once served as a look-out post. If you walk through the old bell tower you will reach a shady plaza from which you can sweep your gaze over the city, the harbour and the Isle St Marguerite.

The Beaches

The Croisette: Twenty seven beaches in all, of which seven are public.
Boulevard du Midi: Nearly 3 miles (4.5km) of public beach.
Boulevard Gazagnaire: Large public beach.

Special Events

January: MIDEM (international record and music market).
February: Mimosa festival; international play festival.
March: Old-timer exhibition.

April: MIP (international TV programming market).
May: International Film Festival.
June: Festival of Cabaret.
July/August: Music evenings in the Le Suquet quarter; *Son et Lumière* on the Lêrins Islands; Bridge Festival; International Fireworks Festival; Regatta; International Commercial Film Festival.
September: International Boat Week.
November: International Dance Festival.
December: Expo Cannes; Festival of Religious Art; Antiques Fair.

Around Cannes

In the tracks of Napoleon; Mougins with its distinguished restaurants; the health-resort town of Grasse, the perfume metropolis; cathedrals and the old quarter; Musée Fragonard; back to Cannes on an exciting route (approximately 25 miles/40km, allow a whole day).

After his return from his Elba exile, Napoleon arrived in Cannes (having started from Golfe Juan) with a few of his trusted men. The next morning he began his arduous march through the Alps to Grenoble. We follow their course as far as Grasse.

Mougins, amidst a delightful landscape reminiscent of Tuscany, is certainly worth a visit—not only for the many excellent restaurants (among them the Moulin de Mougin featuring the cuisine of renowned Chef Roger Vergé; Tel: 93 75 78 24; complete menu around 600FF; located in an old oil-mill) but also because this well-preserved town is among the most beautiful in the region.

Jacques Brel used to live at **71 Rue des Lombards**; the Belgian kings Leopold and Baudoin stayed in the former **Hôtel La Pax**; Yves St Laurent spent his holidays in the **Villa Santa Lucia**, and the Moreaus and Deneuves lived in **La Grâce Dieu**. Picasso spent the last years of his life down the hill from the **Chapelle Notre Dame de la Vie**, which is surrounded by cypresses and olive trees.

Once you've driven past Mouans Sartou you can already begin to make out **Grasse**. The village started as a health resort for the likes of Queen Victoria and Napoleon's sister, Pauline. All manner of gloves—of finest leather—are produced in the shaded streets around the church. After Katherine de Medici imported the trend of wearing perfumed gloves (from Italy), it was a logical step to begin producing the necessary scents in Grasse. In the 18th century there were already several firms which processed mimosa, needle furze, and orange flowers, roses, lavender, jasmine and hyacinths by the ton into minute amounts of concentrated essences. Today Grasse is the most important perfume-making cities in the world.

You can tour the large perfume factories of **Fragonard** (there's a beautiful sculpture by Arman before the entrance), **Galimard** and **Molinard**. If you're not afraid of paying the price, you can also have your very own perfume developed with the help of a perfume 'composer', although this process can take up to three years. You can also study this fine craft at the firm of **Foure Bertrand Dupont**, a private institute in which the most well-versed 'noses' of our time are schooled with exercises on the "scent organ".

The **old city** (this tour lasts about three hours) begins behind the **Cathedral Notre Dame du Puy** (which houses a triptych by Bréa, a Fragonard and three oil paintings by Rubens). The old city is still primarily orientated towards the needs of the locals, which is what makes it particularly interesting for tourists. The

Place aux Aires is especially attractive; every morning a vegetable and flower market is held there.

Jean Honoré Fragonard (1732–1806) was a native of Grasse whose family intended him to become a notary. He had already been awarded the Prix de Rome at the age of 20 and very rapidly advanced to become a fashionable painter of the Paris aristocracy, designing a tapestry for Louis XV. He fell into financial difficulties when the Revolution took its toll on his clientele and had to return to Grasse. Later he eked out a paltry living in Paris until his death. You can examine copies of his work as well as pieces by his son and grandson in the **Musée Fragonard**.

For our trip back to Cannes we will take an especially attractive route. We follow the D4 to Cabris, where many artists have settled. If you are interested in acquiring authentic and locally

A decisive 'nose'

made crèches (nativity figures) or *santons*—figures of saints made out of unfired clay—you should stop in at **18 Rue de la Terrace**. You might also find youself drawn to one of the very simple—and thus especially impressive—carved wooden Madonnas which are made by the son of the house. This would be a lovely, and unusual souvenir of your stay on the Côte.

We continue on the D11 through **Spéradédès** with its mill and wash-houses up to the the D562, which we take towards Draguignon until the D94 branches off to the left—leading us down to the **Auberge St Cassien**. Next to the Auberge, where entire coach-loads of visitors are fed during the high tourist season, there is a captivating chapel dating from the 12th century. If, despite the signs forbidding it, you dare to set foot on the path, you will find a lovely view of a picturesque river valley, a tributary of Lake St Cassien and a rectangular defensive tower with only one window. Perhaps this little tour is worth the risk of innocent trespassing.

At the next intersection we turn left onto the D38, keeping to the right after about a mile (1.5km). Then a narrow road heads off over the little-developed **Tanneron Massiv** (D138) with lovely forests of mimosa and eucalyptus. These were replanted after the huge forest fire of 1970. From Mandelieu we drive onto the heavily travelled RN7 and then back to Cannes.

Cannes → St Tropez

Coast of Red Cliffs

The Esterel mountains; the Théole green zone with yacht harbour and clean beaches; the exclusive sea-side resort of Miramar; the view from the Point de l'Observatoire; St Raphael and the historic neighbouring city of Fréjus (about 28 miles/45km—allow 5 hours).

Massif de l'Esterel

The **Corniche d'Or**, which passes through a landscape of unique beauty, was laid out in 1903 on the initiative of the Touring-Club de France. This section of the coast has a completely different character to that between Menton and Cannes: the backdrop to Nice features the high Alps; here the **Esterel Mountains** are only around 650ft (200m) high, but they are nonetheless imposing, with their red cliffs of volcanic stone.

The landscape is dominated by spruces, pines, chestnuts, eucalyptus trees and cork-oaks; inviting little coves beckon you to take a swim, and there are numerous paths which lead up to the summits—from which you can take in a splendid panorama.

The highest peak is **Mont Vinaigre** (2027ft/618m). In its neighbourhood almost every mailcoach used to be held up and robbed. *"Passer le pas de l'Esterel"* was a long a common expression for an uncomfortable and fatiguing journey. The range is split by deep gorges which continue out to the sea. There the waves break against vertical rock walls, indented capes, minute inlets and

a Sagne
Montblanc
Briançonnet
St.Auban
Le Brunet
La Foux
Valderoure
Séranon
Caille
Esclapon
Mons
Fayence
Tourettes
Le Bégude
Bagnois-
en- Fôret
Puget-sur-
Argens
Les
Tourres
San- Peire-
sur- Mer
La Nartelle

Les Mujouls
Estéron
Gars
Girande
Le Mas
Les Sausses
Aiglun
MONTAGNE DE CHARAMEL

Sigale
Roquesteron
Pierrefeu
Conségudes
Les Ferres
Bonson
Gilette
Bouyon
Le Broc
Carros

MONTAGNE
DU
CHEIRON
Gréolières-
les- Neiges
Cime du Cheiron
1777
Gréolières
Bézaudun-
les- Alpes
Mouton d'Anou
1085

Thorenc
Loup
Estéron
Courségoules
Gattières
Col de Vence
970
St. Barnabé
St. Jeannet
Cipières
Andon
MONTAGNE
DE
L'AUDIBERGUE
St. Maurice
L'Ecre
Courmes
Vence
La Gaude
Caussols
Tourette-
sur- Loup
La
Barenne
Escragnolles
Nans
Gourdon
St. Paul
Le Bar
Loup
Le Colle-
sur- Loup
St.Vallier- de- Thiey
Pas de la Faye
Magagnosc
Rouret
Roquefort-
les- Pins
Cagnes
Grottes de
St.Cézaire
Grasse
Châteauneuf-
Grasse
Les
Maillans
St.Cézaire-
sur-Saigne
Cabris
Plascassier
Biot
Villeneuf-
Loubet-
Plage
Le Tignet
Peymeinade
Valbonne
Sophia-
Antipolis
Zoo marin
Montauroux
Roquefort-
les- Saigne
Mouans-
Sartoux
Tanneron
Mougins
St.Paul-
en- Fôret
Pégomas
St.Jean
Vallauris
Esterel
Lac de
St.Cassien
MASSIF
DU
TANNERON
Le Cannet
Golfe-
Juan
Antibes
Reyran
Mandelieu
Cannes
Golfe Juan
Cap d'Antibes
Les Adrets
de-l'Esterel
L'Eglise
Golfe de Napoule
Ile St.Marguerite
Maure-
Viell
St. Jean
Théole- sur- Mer
Ile St.Honorat
Mont
Vinaigre
618
La Galère
ILES DE LÉRINS
Le Capitou
Miramar
CÔTE D'AZUR
Valescure
Agay
DE
MASSIF
L'ESTEREL
Anthéor Plage
Fréjus
Anthéor
St.Raphaël
Le Dramont
Boulouris
CORNICHE
DE
Cap du Dramont
Golfe de Fréjus
St.Aygulf
La Gaillarde
CÔTE
D'AZUR
Les Issambres
Val d'Esquières

Mediterranean

Sea

**Corniche
de L'Esterel**

8 miles / 12 km

Port-La-Galère

calanques (small natural bays). They also wash up against rocks and little green islands off the coast.

La Napoule, at the foot of Mont San Pieré, is a section of **Mandilieu**—the 'mimosa capital' on the shores of the Siagne. Jean Sablon, the 'French Bing Crosby' has made his home in **Théole** since 1949. Louis Féraud, who gets the inspiration for his wondrously colourful fashion collections here, enthuses: "Here is the cradle of my success, the origin of my creativity."

In antiquity Théole was nothing more than a stop along the route from Nice to Marseille. It was a part of Mandelieu for a long period, not becoming an independent community until the beginning of the 20th century. The first registered Théolien, a librarian, is still alive today. The town is proud of its four yacht harbours with more than 1,000 boats, its 6 miles (10km) of sparkling beaches and 65 miles (102km) of hiking paths in the forested hinterland. Eighty percent of the land belonging to the township has been declared a 'green zone'. Among those who enjoy the peace and quiet here are fashion designer Pierre Cardin, the aircraft builder Serge Dassault and a couple of Emirs (one of whom owns the Hotel Saint Christophe). Richelieu was also attracted to the area—he had a castle built right on the sea when the Spaniards were in possession of the Lêrins Islands. In August the *Nuits de L'Esterel* (concerts and events including folklore presentations and fireworks) are held there.

Above Théole is a villa which appears to consist of bull's-eye windows stacked on top of each other. It was designed by the Hungarian-born Antti Lovag, a student of architect Couelle, for his personal use. The house has neither a roof nor a façade in the traditional

sense. You can easily climb upon the 'red bullets' and hop from one to the other. The vacation settlement, **Port La Galère**, is located in a wooded area on a cliff above the bay of La Napoule. It was created by Couelle, the inventor of 'habitable sculpture'. The peculiar cave-like holes in their exterior walls allow the houses to blend into the cliffs. The beach is one of the most beautiful on the coast, although it is reserved for the residents and guests of the private complex.

The exclusive sea-side resort of **Miramar** has a private yacht harbour in La Figueirette Bay. In the 17th century an abundance of tuna used to be caught in these waters. The first fish farm in the region was established there in 1986; it spawns thirty tons of silver bream and loup per year. The loup seems to be the only resident of this area that suffers from the results of stress: it is said that they have a strong tendency towards heart attacks. Be sure not to miss the splendid view over the red cliffs and blue sea to be had from the **Point de l'Observatoire**. A short way before **Anthéor** you can turn off to the right to the **Pic du Cap Roux**, from which the panorama is equally overwhelming.

The well protected bay of **Agay** was already popular with the Ligurians, Greeks and Romans. The town is overtowered by the 945ft (288m) high **Rastel d'Agay.** There are two impression-rich excursions which can be made from here: take the deserted road through the mountain silence to **Pic de l'Ours**, **Mont Vinaigre** and the **Malpey Ranger Station**—where the elegant criminal boss, Gaspard de Besse, managed his shady business in the 18th century—or take the route to **Valescure**.

Cap Esterel is one of the region's gigantic new projects involving 525 acres (210ha) of land, 1,500 acres (600ha) of forests, two lakes—formed by quarries formed when the railways were being constructed—and 4,000 newly planted trees. These are ideal prerequisites for the new vacation centre, a modern Provençal village of three storey houses. There won't be any cars in the settlement—they will remain in a large parking area outside the complex.

St Raphael, a former health-resort for wealthy families from Fréjus, was the possession of the monks of Lérins in the 10th century; during the 12th century it was in the custody of the Knights Templar. From a distance the martial appearance of the church still conveys an impression of the threats which came here over the sea. Napoleon landed here after his return from Egypt; 14 years later when he was banished to Elba he also departed from here. Alphonse Karr, the widely read chief editor of *Le Figaro* during the 19th century, lived at first in Nice before he discovered St Raphael, and then settled here. He was followed by friends such as Dumas, de Maupassant, Berlioz and Gounod. The latter composed his *Romeo and Juliet* here. Erika Mann described St Raphael as a "stately old-fashioned Riviera town", which, with its palm-lined promenade, numerous hotels and casino, was very popular, especially among the British. Today the city has 30,000 residents, the Santa Lucia convention centre, the 'most beautiful train station in Europe' (reachable from Paris in four hours on the TGV), seven harbours and the **Musée Archéologique** (with a large collection of amphorae) in whose garden stands a Roman milestone from the Via Aurelia.

The neighbouring city of **Fréjus**—Caesar's Forum Julii—was located on an extension of the Via Aurelia which went through Gaul to Spain. Emperor Augustus had galleys built here; he owed his victory over the fleet of Anthony and Cleopatra to their manoeuvrability. Around the time of the birth of Christ this city was—besides Ostia—the largest Roman harbour in the western Mediterranean. Forty thousand people lived within the approximately 2 mile (3km) long city walls. By the way, the **Amphitheatre** was a later addition, built in 1828, and is used today for bullfights and rock concerts. The 25 mile (40km) long **aqueduct** brought water to Fréjus from the River Siagnole near Mons.

The **cathedral district** (a tour takes about 45mins) is in the centre of the present-day city at the Place Formige. It includes a baptistry from the 4th century; a cathedral which dates partly from the 10th century, partly from the 12th, with wings from the late Middle Ages; and the former bishop's palace. To view the **Cité épiscopale** it is best to take a guided tour. Today, despite the modern quarter of Fréjus Plage, Fréjus has more the feel of an inland city. The old harbour gradually silted up and was finally filled in during the 18th century.

The Argens Valley separates the Esterel Massif from the Massif des Maures (the destination of our next tour), which was formed in the same period.

IL EST INTERDIT

De laisser les enfants jouer
avec la fontaine

D'y laver du linge, des autos
motos ou autres engins

En cas d'infraction constatée
la fontaine sera supprimée.

Massif des Maures

The vacation town of St Aygulf; fashionable St Maxime; fish in L'Hermitage; Port Grimaud—'the Venice of Provence' (22 miles/35km; allow 3 hours in the high season).

The **Massif des Maures** was either named after the Moors or is a derivation of the Greek *amauros*, which was corrupted in the Provençal dialect to *maouro* (gloomy or dark). The latter seems more illuminating to me, since dark forests are an essential characteristic of the Massif: oak forests with an underbrush consisting of furzes and myrrh bushes, briars (the roots of which are made into renowned pipes), pine forests, chestnut groves and the cork-oaks whose bark is cut off every seven years to produce bottle corks.

It is beautiful and lonely in these forests, which are interspersed, here and there, by gently rolling hills with olive trees and sheep grazing amid crimson poppies and the occasional field filled with rows of vines. Olives, bread, sheep's cheese and a bottle of good red wine—such a picnic befits the landscape and forms an exquisite pleasure in its simplicity! The contrast between the bustling resort towns and this quiet landscape couldn't be greater. Only a short distance away from the hubbub you feel as though you're in another world. When you have had your fill, return to the coast for a while in order to get as rapidly as possible to St Tropez—aiming to arrive shortly after sunset.

St Aygulf is a little resort town with a sand beach surrounded by cliffs. Even in August you can find your own beautiful corner of the Mediterranean if you go to the trouble of climbing down from the coastal road to the little hidden beaches of **Les Issambres**, **San Peiré**, **Val d'Esquières** and **La Garonette**. This is the perfect place for a late afternoon swim.

The **Gulf of St Tropez** begins at **St Maxime**—where the villas become large again, and we re-enter the land of the obviously rich and famous. This fashionable resort town is picturesquely situated in the north shore of the bay. It includes both fishing boat and yacht harbours as well as a beautiful sandy beach. The restored **old quarter** is reserved for pedestrians in the afternoons during the high season. The monks of Lérins erected the rectangular tower before the harbour for defensive purposes. Later it served as a court building, and today it shelters the **Musée des Traditions Locales**. The **church** has an interesting altar made of green marble which originated in the Charterhouse of La Verne. The choir pew dates from the 15th century.

From grandeur to the profane: the **Casino** was built in 1932. You can see and hear a collection of over 300 musical automatons (unique in Europe) at the **Musée du Phonographe et de la Musique Mécanique**. Guy de Maupassant's family once lived in the villa Béthanie (in the area of the Casino to the left past the Traverse Granier). There isn't much room for boredom in St Maxime with its five night clubs and many different festivals and events (folklore, concerts, galas, fireworks and exhibitions). In **L'Hermitage**, at the harbour, a delicious loup with fennel awaits you.

Port Grimaud is located deep in the interior of the bay. It seemed destined for a similar fate to that of Fréjus: the ancient harbour has been filled in by the swampy delta of the River Giscle. The town hasn't taken this sitting down, however. Like Venice it has had to be ingenious to survive. In 1964, following plans drawn up by the architectural firm Spoerry, construction work began on a new port built on pilings out in the water. Colourfully painted houses with tiled roofs hem the streets, shady little plazas invite us to linger a while, small bridges span the canals on which the *Coches d'eau* (water-coaches) serve as the means of public transport.

Visually, Spoerry orientated the design toward the fishing villages of the Mediterranean region, recapturing an authentic 'spirit of place' although the buildings are adapted to modern living requirements. Each house

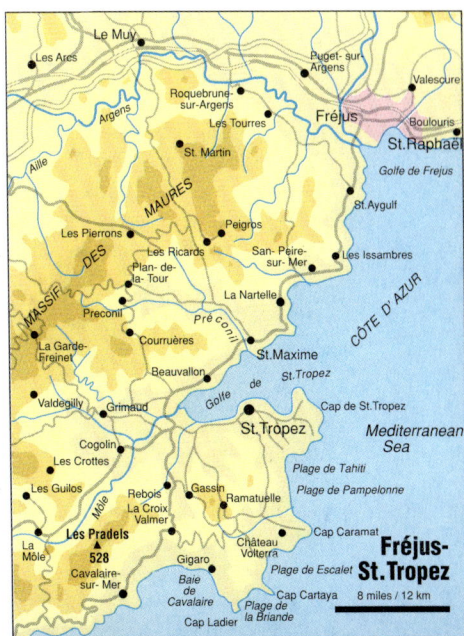

Fréjus-St.Tropez

Port Grimaud

has access to both the street and the water, and it represents an exceptionally successful example of contemporary coastal architecture. A far cry from the concrete and glass horrors lining the Mediterranean elsewhere.

The beautifully restored mediaeval village of **Grimaud** is located below the imposing ruins of its fortress. The serpentine portals and basalt arcades in the **Rue de Templier** are quite impressive. The little Romanesque **Eglise St Michel** is also very pretty.

Outing to La Garde-Freinet

A picturesque Provençal village in an idyllic landscape; shopping in the Maison de la Garde-Freinet; dining amidst nature in La Faucado (about 12 miles/20km; half a day).

La Garde Freinet, formerly named Fraxinet, is situated far into the Maure Massif amidst an area of natural forest. The village, located at an altitude of about 1,300ft (400m) between the fertile Argens Plain and the Gulf of St Tropez, was occupied by the Saracens for over a century. They taught the people of Provence how to use cork-oak and produce pine tar, and they introduced ceramic tiles and the tambourine to the area. They built a strong fortress on the hill above the village which served as the starting point for their plundering raids—until the courageous Count William finally managed to drive the Saracens out permanently in 973AD.

The village is worthy of exploration with its many fountains and little alleyways as well as its Renaissance church and old wash-house.

94

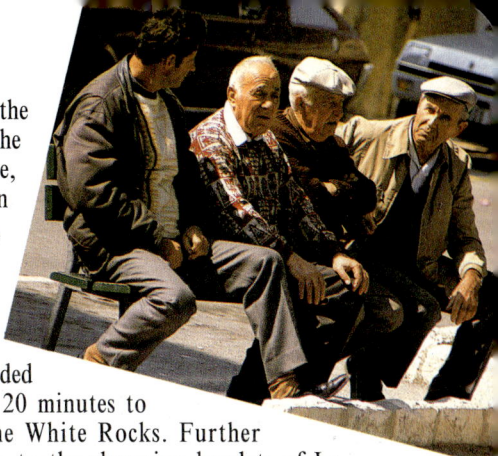

At the entrance of the village is the **Maison de la Garde-Freinet**—the former Chapelle St Eloi—where, alongside handicrafts, you can also buy cheese, honey, wine, preserves and candied sweet chestnuts. The area is a hiker's paradise. The walk up to the fortress ruins takes about half an hour, for which you are rewarded with a splendid view. It takes 20 minutes to get the **Roches Blanches**—the White Rocks. Further hiking excursions can be taken to the charming hamlets of La Mourre, Val de Gilly, Nid du Duc, Bas-Olivier, Camp de la Suyère, Val d'Aubert and Gagnal. A brochure with hiking routes is available at the tourist office. You can enjoy a delightful dining experience amidst nature on the terrace of the **La Faucado** (Tel: 94 43 60 41). The collar-dove ragout and fillet of beef in port wine with morels are especially good.

The famous **Charterhouse of La Verne**, founded in 1170 and abandoned by the monks in 1792, is only 14 miles (23km) away: the most beautiful route is the road to Collobrières; from there we take the D14 through lovely chestnut groves and cork-oak forests in the direction of Grimaud until the rough road to the Charterhouse turns off to the left.

The following festivals of La Garde Freinet have been able to retain much of their original character:

1 May	St Clément Bravade (parade).
Mid-June	Maure Forest festival.
15 August	Village festival in La Mourre with parade.
Late October	Chestnut festival.

The coastline of St Tropez

ST TROPEZ

Den of Iniquity—or Fishing Village?

View from the Citadel, playing boule in the Café des Arts; seeing and being seen in the Sénéquier, the Gorille or Le Café de Paris; typical country dishes in the Lou Revelen, Chez Fuchs or Palmyre (24 hours—if the night turns into day).

If you believe the legend, this port city—located on the southern shore of one of the most beautiful bays on the Côte d'Azur—owes its name to a Roman soldier by the name of Tropez, who was converted to Christianity during the reign of Nero. This cost him his head, in the truest sense of the phrase. His decapitated corpse was placed in a boat with a dog and a rooster (which were supposed to devour it) and abandoned to the waves. However, miraculously, it landed undamaged on the beach of present-day St Tropez.

In memory of the martyr, the *Bravade* takes place every year on 16 May—a spectacular and very loud procession in which a gilded wooden bust of the saint is carried throughout the city, inspiring the faithful and entertaining all others. The second *Bravade*, on 15 of June, commemorates the year 1637 when the people of St Tropez fended off an attack by 22 Spanish galleons which were attempting to plunder the town and capture the four royal ships anchored in the harbour. At the end of the 19th century, Guy de Maupassant wrote of this sleepy fishing village: "What an enchanting and simple daughter of the sea! You can smell the fishcatch, the burning tar, the brine. The scales of sardines glitter on the cobblestones like pearls." Quite a lot has change since then, but the enchantment remains to this day.

Paul Signac, who came here to paint, was so enchanted with the town that he decided to stay. He bought the estate called La Hune and invited many painters to come and visit: Matisse, Marquet, Bonnard, Picabia, Van Dongen, Utrillo and Dufy, to name only a few. Their works are exhibited in the **Musée de l'Annonciade** (Place Grammont). In 1925, Colette, the author—who was then considered rather indelicate—settled on the peninsula. As early as 1907 she had appeared topless in a Paris theatre. Neither did she hesitate to swim nude in the sea before her house, the Treille Muscate. (Perhaps the author, who started out as a music hall actress, was merely expressing a *joie de vivre* repressed during her years as Willy Gauthier-Villars' slave-with-a-pen.)

Not long after, the first night clubs for rich tourists were established. The village then grew fashionable. Swashbuckler Errol Flynn and author and diarist Anaïs Nin—one of Henry Miller's muses—were regular guests. After World War II, Jean Cocteau and the Paris literary scene washed up on the shore. Somewhat later came the unforgettable Juliette Gréco as well as countless actors, directors and other show business people. Brigitte Bardot bought the La Madrague estate only 1,000ft (300m) away from Colette's former residence. The authoress sold her house in 1938; BB still lives here today with her many pets, this despite the invasion of tourists. In the month of August alone more than 80,000 visit St Tropez, a town which has only 6,250 residents during the winter.

Brigitte Bardot isn't the only person who has stayed

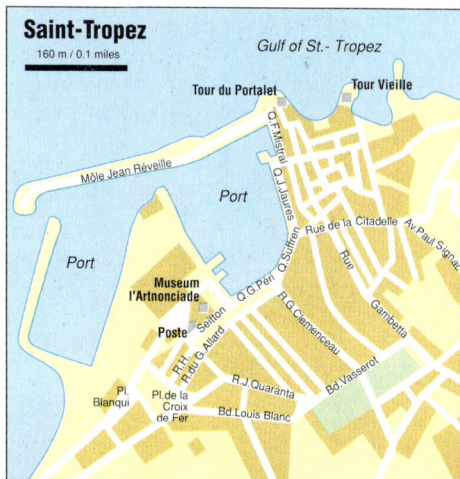

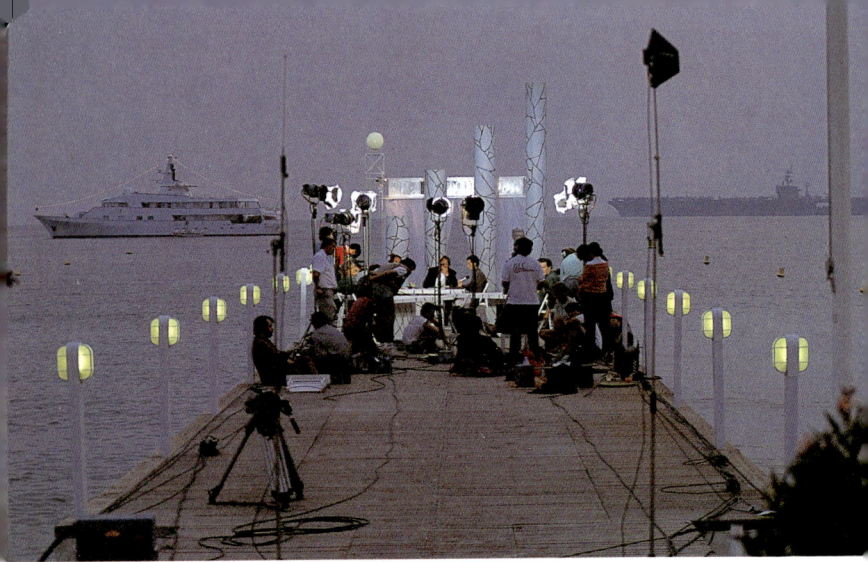

Only on the Côte d'Azur...

in St Tropez: the film director Roger Vadim—who was already familiar with the village before he met Bardot—spends three months here every year and lives with one of his numerous ex-wives; Jean-Pierre Aumont, Hollywood's 'French Lover' and writer, acquired a taste for the village when he visited Colette; he still lives above the bay in his villa San Genesto today.

The reasons are simple: St Tropez possesses a charm of its very own—and always will, since it is something indelible which cannot be destroyed. Whatever the time of day or year, when you come in from St Maxim the pastel-hued buildings (reconstructed following the original designs after being destroyed in 1944) seem to lose themselves between the sky and the sea. One can immediately understand why so many painters came here and were inspired by their surroundings, and why so many who came here have been inspired to paint for the first time..

If you climb up the hills to the **citadel** at sunset and take in the view of the bay, the harbour and the town with its narrow alleyways and the grey-green tower of the church, then you will

recognize the 'colourful shadows' which so fascinated Bonnard. Also, down in the village you will meet the 'Tropézians' since—despite all the rumours—there are still some remaining: at the authentic fish-market in the area of the quay; in the cafés with their old mirrors and worn-out table tops; in the **Rue de la Miséricorde** with its arcades; in the **Rue Allard** and on the **Place aux Herbes**.

Fish used to be cleaned underneath the shade of the plane-trees at the **Place des Lices**; now a market is held there on Tuesdays and Saturday mornings and the native residents play *boule* with the *coco parisien du showbiz* (an affectionate but ironic designation for Parisian show-business people). If you want to stay well-informed, listen to Radio St Tropez (89.5FM): *L'Invité du Jour* at 12.35pm and *Le Club des Stars* at 7pm. St Tropez still has 15 fishing boats which make daily deliveries to the restaurants and the little fish market—thus preserving its status as a fishing village. However, in summer the work of the fishermen is not made any easier by the plethora of yachts.

St Tropez would not be what it is today without the **Sénéquier**, **Le Gorille** and **Le Café de Paris**—the 'in' places on the harbour. If you want to pass as a native, then enter the terrace of the **Sénéquiers** from the rear. Here the prominent and the prettiest girls meet together in the mornings between 11am and noon. Henri Guerin Jr is the champion of the steak tartare with french fries—20 tons are consumed in **Le Gorille**, which even in the 1950s was staying open around the clock. André Moraud and his son pour in the region of 45 gallons (200 litres) of beer per day!

La Cave Coopérative has an annual production of 11,000 hectolitres (290,589 gallons) of wine, of which 7,000 are classified as Côtes de Provence AOC. That's 450,000 bottles per year, primarily of rosé—the wine of summer. However, there is also an especially

good red, the *Cuvée des Bravades* (for further information contact the tourist office on 94 97 45 21).

Due to the fact that in summer you can only reach the village through interminable traffic jams, there is also a **mini-airport** only a few steps away from the village centre. It serves a helicopter line between St Tropez and the Nice airport. Of course it's not cheap.

You can get typical country dishes at **Lou Revelen** (4 rue des Ramparts; Tel: 94 97 06 34) in the old Quartier de la Ponche—only a couple of strides from the City Hall. The **Chez Fuchs** in the Rue Commercants (7 rue des Commercants; Tel: 94 97 01 25) is very popular for its *plat du jour*. The restaurant **Palmyre** (2 rue Petit-Bal; Tel: 94 97 43 22) is located in the heart of St Tropez, but it has country charm. **Chez Nano** (Tel: 94 97 91 66) directly opposite the city hall, also lures visitors with its *plat du jour:* traditional cuisine which owes its excellence to use of the freshest produce. It is imperative that you make reservations at all these restaurants.

By the way, the least expensive double room is to be had at **Les Lauriers** (Rue de Temple; Tel: 94 97 04 88). This ochre-hued villa is located just behind the Place des Cices. On the other hand, the most beautiful hotel is certainly **La Ponche** (Place de Revelin; Tel: 94 97 02 53) in the old fishing quarter.

The Beaches

Plage des Graniers: Easily reached on foot.
Bay of Canébeirs: With steep cliffs.
Tamaris Beach: In the region of Brigitte Bardot's villa.
Plage des Salins: 2½ miles (4km) east of St Tropez (from there you can take an attractive footpath around the peninsula).

Plage de Tahiti: Gained its name after being used as the Tahitian set for a film directed by René Clair; it belongs to Ramatuelle village.
Plage de Pampelonne: A 3 mile (5km) long beach of fine sand; also belonging to Ramatuelle.
Plage de L'Escalet: Cliffs and sand.
Plage de la Bastide Blanche: Only accessible via a bad road, but very popular.

Where the Crickets Chirp

The La Croix Valmer resort; along the coast to Cap Taillat and its beach; the Provençal village of Gassin; the view from the mills of Paillas; a secret tip; the village of Ramatuelle (a round-trip of about 25 miles/40km; roughly 3 hours).

Departing from St Tropez you take the D98a to La Foux and then turn left onto the N559. Because of its mild climate, **La Croix Valmer** has become a popular health resort. Gently rolling hills overgrown with oaks, pines and eucalyptus trees protect the village and the stately villas from cold winds, also helping the quality of the wines cultivated here. The attractive Bouillabaise Beach is overcrowded during the summer. The path along the coast to Cap Taillat is a good tip.

Gassin is a typical Provençal village, located a commanding 650ft (200m) above the Gulf of St Tropez. **Les Moulins des Paillas** were still serving their functions as mills until the turn of the century; are now a popular destination for outings.

Ramatuelle, idyllically located on a height surrounded by vineyards, is a little known secret for all those who find St Tropez too crowded. The village has been shaped by three historical events: the occupation by the Saracens in AD892, almost total destruction in 1592 because of religious conflicts between Catholics and the Protestant Henry IV; and World War II.

Jean Pierre Aumont, mentioned earlier, was sought out because of his knowledge of English by the Americans forces landing on Pampelonne to help make contact with the *Resistance Ramatuellois*, and so the residents of Cavalaire, La Croix-Valmer and Cogolin had a chance to see their film idol in person—in a Jeep surrounded by GIS. Today, on the other hand, the actor Jean Claude Brialy creates quite a furore as the artistic director of the **Festival Gérard Philipe**, which has been held annually since 1984 (Philipe's grave is in the Ramatuelle cemetery; the book his wife wrote about the last months they spent together is well worth reading). Brialy knows how to combine work and pleasure in a most admirable manner: an apartment in one of the twisting alleyways, breakfast in the **Café des Ormeaux**; dinner in the **Plage Vert** or the **Mooréa**.

Those who know the 'naked facts' of the local beaches would scarcely be surprised to learn that 'Emmanuelle'—alias Sylvia Kristel—has settled near Pampelonne Beach with her husband.

Now we follow the D61, then turn left onto the D93, which leads along the vineyards above Pampelonne Bay. The **Chapelle St Anne** is located in the shade of huge trees on a volcanic cone to our right. The little road, into which we make a right turn to reach the chapel, leads back to St Tropez.

POSTES

HEURES DES LEVÉES

JOURS OUVRABLES

11H

SAMEDI

10H

BUREAU
LE PLUS PROCHE

ST.PAUL

NE PAS JETER DE JOURNAUX
DANS CETTE BOITE

Dining Exper

Jacques Mèdecin, once the most powerful man in the region, is also the author of a cook book (*The Cuisine of Nice*), which just goes to show what an important rôle the kitchen plays in French society. The former mayor of Nice ended his political career in September 1990—he resigned and disappeared to South America. I can't judge the merit of the warrant that has been issued for his arrest, but his cook book can hold its ground against any criticism.

Fortunately, after a recent, but thankfully brief, flirtation with Nouvelle Cuisine, the top chefs of the Côte—of which there are quite a few—have returned to the traditional regional recipes. In order to help you decipher the menu, and make the most of the local cuisine, several of the best specialities are listed below.

Pissaladiera is a delectable onion cake, flavoured with sardine purée (pissala) and local black olives. **Socca** is a type of thin pancake made of garbanzo bean flour. For **Ratatouia** the individual vegetables (tomatoes, aubergines, peppers, and courgettes) are cooked separately and shouldn't be mixed together until just

before serving. **Tourte de Bléa** is a salty pie which is filled with beet greens, currants and almonds or pine nuts.

Salade Niçoise, if properly prepared, must consist of salad greens, cucumber slices, tomatoes, black olives, hard-boiled eggs, onions, tuna fish and anchovy filets.

The **Mesclun** is a hearty-tasting salad which absolutely must include dandelion and hedge-mustard leaves. **Petit Farcis** are artichoke hearts, baby courgettes and tomatoes with a spicy minced-meat filling which are served *gratinée*. The delicious **beignets des courgettes** are courgette flowers dipped in butter and deep fried, a true delicacy, and one of the world's rare flavours. **Tripe à la Niçoise** is prepared with tomatoes, carrots and lots of garlic. It is the one tripe dish that even dedicated adversaries should taste. **Stocaficada** is a stew of

dried codfish—trying it takes a good deal more courage.

Everything which has **Pistou** in its name has to do with basil, the ubiquitious herb of the mediterranean summer. For example, a vegetable soup is transformed when a paste of basil, garlic and olive oil is added. This is equally true of pâtés and pasta. The latter is mixed with pistou and topped off with parmesan cheese. **Gnocchi, ravioli and pizza** taste just as good here as in Italy. **Daube** is large cubes of beef cooked until tender over a low flame in red wine with cinnamon and lemon peel. **Pan bagnat**—white bread soaked with olive oil and layered with greens, onions, tomatoes, hard-boiled eggs and tuna fish—are also sold on the beaches and are a refreshing delicacy in the heat of the mid-afternoon. **Violets** are the small young artichokes without which no crudité basket is worth its name; they are eaten raw. **Aioli** is a garlic-flavoured mayonnaise; it is served on Fridays with boiled fish and vegetables, a gesture to the days of the Catholic past when everyone ate fish on Friday.

Soup de Poisson is a clear fish broth; you eat it in the following manner: rub the croutons with the garlic cloves that are served with them, lay them in the dish, place a spoonful of the delectable **rouille** (mayonnaise with garlic and pimentos) on top, sprinkle cheese over it and finally pour the soup on top of the lot. On the other hand, really well-prepared **bouillabaise**, a medley of fish and flavours, is only found in a few restaurants—even though it is the most famous regional speciality. Because it involves numerous fresh ingredients it is not cheap, or easy to make—but it's a pleasure you shouldn't deny yourself.

The tastiest Mediterranean fish are **loup**, **St Pierre**, **silver bream** and the red **rougets**; the latter should only be ordered filleted, since they have an unbelievable number of bones. **Mussels** and **shellfish** should only be eaten from September to April unless you know the restaurant *very* well.

The **lamb** in this area bears no resemblance whatsoever to the strong-smelling mutton stew which has ruined the pleasure of many in this delicious meat. Since the sheep eat the herbs and spices of Provence the dishes (such as **Gigot**—leg of lamb, and **Agneau de Sisteron**) taste simply marvellous.

Wine

Provence is famous for its rosé wines, which form the greater portion of the overall production. It should always be drunk ice cold. Rosés are made of purple or red grapes fermented without the skin. **Côtes de Provence** produces AOC—Appelation d'Origine Contrôlée—wines (Bandol, Bellet, Cassis, Palette) which vary from good to rather plain country wines (particularly reds). AOC is a controlled designation of origin which—within a certain region—regulates the types of grapes, the maximum output, the minimum alcohol content and the number of vines per given area. On the label either the name of the region is printed in large letters along with the words *Appelation Contrôlée*, or the words surround the region, for example: *Appellation Bandol Contrôlée*. VDQS means *Vin Délimité de Qualité Supérieure* and denotes wines of better quality from certain precisely defined areas. These *qualité* wines rank just behind the AOC's under French law.

Recommended wines to drink with fish, shellfish and mussel dishes are **Cassis** (a dry, first-class AOC white wine from Cassis in the area of Marseille), **Bellet** (a very dry yet fruity AOC white wine from the area of Nice), **Palette** (an AOC white wine from the area of Aix-en-Provence) or a white **Bandol**. There are a huge selection of red wines. Those of **Bandol** and the north side of the **Maure Massif** are rounded and hearty, while the elegant and finer ones come from **St Tropez** and the **Argens Valley**. The most popular wines come from the following areas: **Bandol, Ollioules, Pierrefeu, Cuers, Taradeau, La Croix Valmer** and—in the area around Nice—**Bellet, La Gaude, St Jeannet** and **Menton**.

Domaine means that the wine comes from vineyards which may extend over several counties. **Château** means a castle or estate winery. If the label indicates that the bottling of the wine was done directly on a domaine or at a castle, then you can be reasonably certain it is a quality wine. **Vin de pays** is a simple wine of the region, including: **vin ordinaire**, table wine; **vin rouge**, red wine; **vin blanc**, white wine and **vin en pichet**, wine served in a jug or a carafe. Wines from the following vineyards, many of which can be visited, are sold throughout the region:

Bellet
CHATEAU DE BELLET, St Roman de Bellet
CHATEAU DE CREMAT, G F A Bagnisfils
CHATEAU DE CALISSANNE, Route départmentale 10 Lancon-de-Provence

Bandol
DOMAINE OTT (rosé)
CHATEAU PRADEAU, St Cyr-sur-Mer (red)
DOMAINE DE PIBARNON, La Cadière d'Azur
MAS DE LA ROUVIERE/MOULIN DES COSTES, La Cadière d'Azur
CHATEAU VANNIERES, between La Cadière d'Azur and St Cyr-sur-Mer

DOMAINE LE GALANTIN, Le Plan dun Castellet
DOMAINE DES SALETTES, La Cadière d'Azur
DOMAINE DE TERREBRUNE, Ollioules

Côtes de Provence
CHATEAU MINUTY, Gassin
DOMAINE BARBEYROLLES, Route de Ramatuelle, Gassin
DOMAINE D'ASTROS, near Vidauban
DOMAINE DES BASTIDES, Le Puy St Réparade
DOMAINE DE L'AUMÉRADE, Pierrefeu
DOMAINE DE LA BASTIDE BLANCHE, Route de l'Escalet, Ramatuelle

Cassis
CLOS ST MAGDALAINE, Avenue du Revestel, Cassis

Coteaux d'Aix
CHATEAU DU SEUIL, Aix-en-Provence
COMANDERIE DE LA BARGEMONE, RN7, St Cannat
CHATEAU VIGNELAURE, Route de Jonques, Rians

Beverages

Coffee and tea aficionados, and the great unwashed thirsty, will make good use of the following catalogue, which takes all the confusion, but none of the variety, out of ordering beverages in France: **café noir** is black coffee served in small cups; **café crème** is coffee with steamed milk, served in medium-sized cups; **café au lait** is coffee with a lot of steamed milk; **café décaféiné** is, not surprisingly, decaffeinated coffee. **Thé au citron** is tea with lemon; **thé au lait** is tea with milk; **tisane** is herbal tea; **infusion de camomile** is camomile tea; **infusion de menthe** is peppermint tea. The French for beer is **bière**; **bière blonde** is light beer or lager; **bière brune** is dark beer; **bière à la pression** is draught beer; **un bock** is a small glass of beer and **panaché**: beer with soda.

Calendar of Special Events

January

Mandelieu: Mimosa festival.
Monaco: Festival of St Devota (Monaco's patron saint). On the evening of 26 January a boat is set ablaze in front of the Devota Church; 27 January sees the Monaco Auto-Rally.
Cannes: MIDEM—international music business exposition/market.

February

Cannes: Mimosa festival.
Menton: Lemon festival (the two weeks around Shrove Tuesday).
Valbonne: Olive and grape festival.
Nice: Carnival; begins three weeks before Shrove Tuesday (*Mardi Gras*) and ends on Ash Wednesday.

March

Nice: Cougourdon folklore festival in Cimiez.
Roquebrune/Cap Martin: Good Friday evening sees the Procession of the Dead Christ.
Antibes/Juan-Les-Pins: Antiques fair.
Vennes: Easter Sunday and Monday: Provençal folklore with flower parade.
Fréjus: Third weekend after Easter—*Bravade* in honour of St Francis.

April

Cannes: International Antiques Fair.
Monaco/Nice International Tennis Tournament.

May

Cannes: International Film Festival.
Nice: Annual parish fair in Cimiez.
Grasse: Provençal folklore, second weekend in May; Rose Festival.
St Tropez: 16–18: *Bravades*.
Monaco: Sunday after Ascension Day: Grand Prix de Monaco (Formula 1).

June

St Tropez: 15: Spaniard *Bravade*.
Nice: Religious music festival.
Cannes: *Festival de Café Théâtre Haut pays en Fête*.

July

Nice: The Great Jazz Parade; International folklore festival; flower battle.
Le Cannet: Flower parade.

Cagnes Sur Mer: Evening trotting-race at the Hippodrom de la Côte d'Azur.
Antibes/Juan Les Pins: World Jazz Festival.
Cannes: Musical evenings in the Suquet Quarter.
Menton: musical evenings in Pian Park.
Les Nuits Des Lerins: *Son et lumiére* on the island of St Marguerite (until mid-September).
Cap D'Antibes: Mariners' procession to the Garoup Church.
Monaco: Concert in the castle court; international firework festival.

July

St Tropez: Musical evening in the Citadel.
Villefranche: Evening performances in the Citadel.

August

Grasse: First Sunday: Jasmine Festival.
Cannes: Fireworks festival.
Roquebrune/Cap Martin: Procession through the old quarter.
Menton: Chamber music festival (on the plaza of St Michael's Church).

September

Cannes: Old-timer Festival (antique cars).
Pielle: First Sunday: festival commemorating the ending of a great water shortage.
St Tropez: La Nioulargue (international sailing competition).

October

Nice: Golf tournament; triathlon.

November

Nice: Golf tournament; 'Sea, Mountain and Leisure' fair; antiques fair, furniture and interior design fair.

December

Nice: Golf tournament; Christmas swim in the sea.
Monaco: International Circus Festival.
Lucéram: 24th: Shepherds' Christmas (to the sound of tambourines and pipes, blessing of the lambs and fruits).

What to Know!

Practical Information

GETTING AROUND

Railway Stations (SNCF)
Nice: Tel: 93 87 50 50.
Cannes: Tel: 93 99 50 50.
Marseille: Tel: 91 08 50 50.

Airports
Nice: Tel: 93 83 91 03.
Marseille: Tel: 91 89 90 10.

Helicopter Service
Héli Air Monaco/Héliport de Monaco
Tel: 93 30 80 88.
Aérogares Nice
Tel: 93 21 34 95.
Héliport de St Tropez
Tel: 94 97 15 123.
Héli St Tropez
Tel: 94 97 59 52.
Héli Transport
Nice: Tel: 93 21 42 00.
Cannes: Tel: 93 43 11 11/93 47 25 51.

USEFUL INFORMATION

Business Hours
Large department stores and shopping centres are open from 10am–noon and 3–7pm, Monday–Saturday. Most food stores are closed from 12.30–4pm. Shops on the market streets are open on Sunday and holidays until 12.30pm. Many of these are closed on Monday. State museums are closed Tuesday and holidays; churches are frequently closed from noon–2pm.

Electrical Equipment
Local current is 220 Volts. Some old sockets require an adaptor (*adapteur*) purchased in electrical stores.

Tipping
Gratuities are, as a rule, included in the final total in hotels, restaurants and cafés; nonetheless it is usual to give an extra *pourboire*. Barbers and hair stylists, taxi drivers, porters and doormen expect to receive a small tip.

Annual Sales
Winter: 2 January–28 February.
Summer: 15 July–15 September.

MONEY MATTERS

Banks
In general, banks are open Mondays–Fridays from 8:30–noon and 1.30–4.30pm. Travellers' cheques and Eurocheques can only be cashed with a passport or other form of personal identification.

The following *Bureaux de Change* are also open on Sunday and holidays: **Bureau de l'Agence Cook** in the Nice railway station, the **Bureau de Change de l'Aeroport de Nice** and the **Office Provençal** (Nice, 10 Rue de France).

Credit Cards

American Express, Carte Bleue, Eurocard, Diners Club, Mastercard and Visa are the most frequently honoured. You can't pay with plastic in the markets and in many small hotels and restaurants.

COMMUNICATIONS & MEDIA

Telephone

You can make local and long distance calls from all post offices and telephone booths. In most public telephone booths this is only possible with a telephone card; these are available in various values at all post offices and many tobacco shops. The local area code forms part of all French telephone numbers (the first two digits). The Alpes Maritime Départment has the code 93; the code for the Départment

Var is 94.

Post Offices (PTT)

The *Bureaux de Poste* are open Monday–Friday from 8am to 7pm; Saturday from 8am–noon. Postage stamps are also available in tobacco shops.

Newspapers and Magazines

Nice Matin is the regional daily newspaper. You can also get the *Interna-tional Herald Tribune* in the morning. Foreign language newspapers are available in the afternoon. *La Semaine et des Spectacles (7 jours/7 nuits)* is a weekly guide to events and performances. Two free classified-ad magazines distributed in various shops are the *06* and the *Super Hebdo*.

Radio Stations

France Musique	94.4Mhz
Radio Baie des Anges	96.8Mhz
Radio France Côte d'Azur	101.4Mhz
Fun Radio	91.9Mhz
Radio Monte Carlo Classique	104Mhz

PUBLIC HOLIDAYS

1 January	New Year's Day
Easter Monday	Moveable feast
1 May	Labour Day
8 May	Armistice Day (1945)
Ascension	Moveable feast
Pentecost	Moveable feast
14 July	Bastille Day
15 August	Assumption
1 November	All Saints' Day
11 November	Armistice Day (1918)
25 December	Christmas Day

EMERGENCIES

Police: Dial 17
Fire Department: Dial 18
Emergency Medical Service
Tel: 93 92 55 55

ON THE ROAD

Driving

The use of safety belts is mandatory. Motorcycle riders must wear helmets. **Speed Limits:** in-town 60kmh (38 mph); on normal roads 90kmh (56 mph); on superhighways (*autoroutes*) 130kmh (80mph). The *autoroutes* are generally toll roads. If you have coins follow the signs reading *automatique*.

Note: there are old and new 10-franc coins. The major automats are already re-equipped to accept the new. In the case of accidents which only involve damage to property, try to avoid a shouting match and fill out the *constat amable* insurance form. It should be noted that the price of petrol is very high in France.

Maps

The best map of the region is Michelin map No 195, Côte d'Azur/Alpes Maritimes, 1/100,000 scale.

ACCOMMODATION

Hotels

The individualists among you will prize the smaller hotels since they have a more personal touch. My selection is limited to such hotels, since they have a special ambience. Lists of hotels with prices and information are

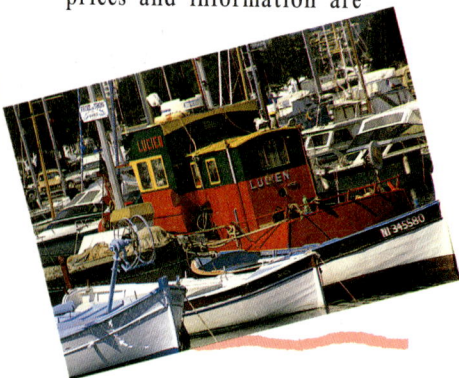

available at tourist offices.
They are divided into five categories:
☆☆☆☆☆ Top class luxury hotel
☆☆☆☆ Luxury hotel
☆☆☆ Very comfortable hotel
☆☆ Comfortable hotel
☆ Moderate hotel
The majority of rooms are still furnished with a *grand lit*—a large double-bed. Since you pay for the room and not for the number of persons staying, two people can visit for the price of one. Most small and medium-sized hotels have no television in the rooms. The *Guide des Auberges et Hotels de Campagne*, with some 350 addresses throughout France, is recommended for fans of small hotels and country guest-houses.

Antibes
Auberge Provençal, 61 Place Nationale. Tel: 93 34 13 24.
Five rooms; 250-480FF.

Cannes
Hotel Villa Toboso. Tel: 93 38 20 05.
Five minutes from the centre; 15 rooms with bath. 300–550FF without breakfast.

Biot
Galerie des Arcades. Tel: 93 65 01 04.
12 rooms with bath or shower. 180–350ff without breakfast.

Vence
La Ferme. Tel: 93 58 74 87.
Four rooms with shower. 450FF with breakfast.

Nice
La Perouse. Tel: 93 62 34 63.
475–975ff without breakfast.
Petit Palais. Tel: 93 62 19-11.
300–450ff without breakfast.

St Maxime
Mas es Brugassieres.
Tel: 94 43 72 42.
11 rooms with bath; 390-590FF.

Grimaud
La Boulangerie. Tel: 94 43 23 16.
11 rooms with bath. 250–395FF without breakfast.

Villefranche sur Mer
Hotel Welcome. Tel: 93 55 27 27.
32 rooms with bath. 468–740FF with breakfast.
Les Olivettes. Tel: 93 01 14 46.

19 rooms with bath. 275–600FF without breakfast.

St Paul de Vence
Le Hameau. Tel: 93 32 80 24.
17 rooms with bath. 240–540FF without breakfast.

St Jean Cap Ferrat
Brise Marine. Tel: 93 76 04 36.
15 rooms with bath. 220-530FF without breakfast.

Mougins
Le Manoie de l'Etang.
Tel: 93 90 01 07.
13 rooms with bath. 450-750FF without breakfast.

Menton
La Bergerie. Tel: 93 04 00 39.
14 rooms with bath. 330FF without breakfast.

St Tropez
La Tartame. Tel: 94 97 21 23.
12 rooms with bath. 550–780FF without breakfast.

Le Pre de la Mer. Tel: 94 97 12 23.
Three rooms with bath. 400–500FF without breakfast. Nine studios with small kitchens; 600FF.

SHOPPING

Nice
In the city centre surrounding the **Place Masséna**, 64 luxury boutiques have come together and designated their neighborhood the **Carré d'As** (look for the blue-green sign: *Bienvenue au Carré d'As*). They've made quality and outstanding service their bywords. The Avenue Jean Médecin is the main business street; it includes the Galleries Lafayette and Nice Etoile. Similarly expensive shops are found in the pedestrian zone in the Rue Masséna/Rue de France. A flea market is held on Monday on the Cours Saleya

between the old quarter and the sea. The imposing shopping centre CAP 3000 is located just behind the airport. It has countless boutiques—for every budget and taste. In **Colle sur Loup** there is a street full of antique shops; the boutiques of **Juan-les-Pins** are open until 11pm. You can buy beautiful glasses in **Biot** in the Verrerie de Biot. Those who like lithography should take a look at the Fondation Maeght in **St Paul de Vence**.

Cannes
The **Rue d'Antibes**—parallel to the Croisette—is the main business street of Cannes. It is often compared with the Rue de Faubourg St Honoré, and the price are just as inflated here as they are there. Each Saturday there is a flea market with relatively reasonable prices in the **Allées de la Liberté** across from the new festival performance house. The **Rue Meynadier** is well known for its good food stores. You can get *eau de toillette* and good soap in **Grasse**, and those who are already thinking of Christmas despite the lovely sunshine can buy nativity figures and statues of saints made of unfired clay—the so-called *santons*—in **Cabris** at 18 Rue de la Terrace. Picasso made Vallauris famous as a pottery centre; you can buy beautiful majolica in the Galerie Madoura.

Ceramics
Annelise Schäle, Rue du Calre, 83440 Seillans.
Phillippe Gallot, Poterie du Boutau, Place de la Liberté,
06720 Levens.
Jean-Luc Feltrini, Grés d'Art, 6 Boulevard de la Republique,
04120 Castellane.
Martine Crochet, 83330 Le Plan du Castellet.
Jean-Pierre Faucher, Saint Eloi, 83131 Montferrat.
Patrick Groman, Rue de la Breche,

30350 Lezan.
Albrecht Schönerstedt, Sculptures Céramiques, Pont du Caramy, 83570 Carces.
Kristie Kammarström, 83131 Montferrat.
Voelkel S & P, 83640 St Zacherie.
Roland Moreau, La Barbacasse, Tourettes sur Loup.

RESTAURANTS

Visiting restaurants on the Côte is a genuine pleasure whether it be a gourmet temple or a simple bistro. The relevant guides with which any gourmet is familiar give information on the countless possible ways to spend a pleasurable evening, although personal recommendations are just as welcome (if not more so) to the dining enthusiast. The following list is a compilation of my own favourite restaurants. Don't forget to make reservations, especially in high season.

Nice
La Merenda, 4 Rue de la Terrasse.
No telephone; small, unassuming bistro with Provençal specialities.
Les Denta de la Mer, 2 Rue St Françoise de Paule. Tel: 93 80 99 16.
Terrace; fish specialities.
L'Eequinade, 5 Quai Deux-Emmanuels. Tel: 93 89 59 36.
Directly on the old harbour; a cheerful ambience; features fish specialities and great desserts; not cheap.

Cannes
La Villa Dionysos, 7 Rue Marceau.
Tel: 93 39 79 73.
Provençal specialities.
Astoux et Brun, 27 Rue Félix Faure.
Tel: 93 39 21 87.
A seafood orgy at reasonable prices.

St Jeannet
Auberge de St Jeannet.
Tel: 93 24 90 06.

Rustic ambience, Mediterranean specialities.

Antibes
Restaurant du Bacon, Boulevard du Bacon. Tel: 93 61 50 02.
Terrace; the best fish restaurant on the Côte; expensive.
Au Régal, 5 Rue Sade.
Tel: 93 34 11 69.
Beautiful garden; very good food.
Auberge Provençale, 61 Place Nationale. Tel: 93 34 13 24.
Beautiful garden in the patio; traditional dishes.

Cagnes-sur-Mer
Charlot, 87 Boulevard de la Plage/ Cros de Cagnes. Tel: 93 31 00 07.
Serene ambience; very good fish dishes.
Le Picadéro, 3 Boulevard de la Plage/ Cros de Cagnes. Tel: 93 73 57 81.
Bistro atmosphere; excellent food.

Juan-les-Pins
Auberge de l'esterel, 21 Chemin des Iles. Tel: 93 61 86 55.
Beautiful garden; outstanding food.

Biot
Galerie des Arcades, 15 Place des Arcades. Tel: 93 65 01 04.
Simple country guest-house.
Auberge du Jarrier, 30 Passage de la Bourgade. Tel: 93 63 11 68.
Terrace; extraordinary food.

Valbonne
Le Bistrot de Valbonne, 11 Rue de la Fontaine. Tel: 93 42 05 59.
A small terrace; excellent food.

Vence
La Farigoule, 15 Rue Henri Isnard.
Tel: 93 58 01 27.
Attractive interior courtyard; Provençal specialities.

Grasse
Mâitre Bosco, 13 Rue de la Fouette.
Tel: 93 36 45 76.

Traditional cuisine at reasonable prices.

St Tropez
Baou-Baou, Plage de la Bouillabaise. Tel: 94 97 18 34.
The chicken with crayfish is especially good.
Le Bistrot des Lices, 3 Place des Lices. Tel: 94 97 29 00.
Meeting place for 'chic' Parisians.
La Marjolaine, Rue Francois Sibile. Tel: 94 97 04 60.
A rustic *trattoria*; I especially recommend the *prix fixé* menu for 98FF.

St Paul de Vence
Le Bougainvillier, 7 Rempart Ouest. Tel: 93 32 89 30.
The owner is the former *maître* of the Colombe d'Or; small, but excellent.
Colombe d'or, Tel: 93 32 80 02.
Romantic terrace; illustrious clientele.

Menton
Chez Germaine, 46 Promenade de Maréchel Le-Clerc. Tel: 93 35 66 90.
Very good salmon with sorrel.

Haut-de-Cagnes
Des Peintres. Tel: 93 20 83 08.
The crayfish and salad with roast duck or goose liver are recommended.
Josey Joe. Tel: 93 20 68 76.
Garden terrace; excellent food.

Antibes/Juan-les-Pins
Le Bureau, Avenue Galies; Juan-les-Pins. Disco; opens at 11.30pm; admission 90FF.
La Siesta, La Brague, Route du Bord de Mer
Seven dance floors; admission 130FF.
Whisky a Gogo, Juan-les-Pins.
Disco; opens at 11pm; admission 40FF.

Cannes
Club Otero, 48 La Croisette; Carlton Hotel. Piano bar/disco
Galaxy, Palais de Festival
Night club; opens at 11pm.
Mogambo/Palm Beach, Point de la Croisette. Restaurant/club/disco.

Nice
Le Baccara Piano Bar, 1 Promenade des Anglais. Open from 11pm–2am.
Centre Ville, 1 Place Massena.
Disco; opens at 10.30pm.
Jok-Club Disco, 1 Promenade des Anglais. Opens at 11pm.
Offshore, 29 Rue Alphonse Karr.
Disco opens at 11pm; admission 100FF.
Au Pizzaiolo, 4 Rue du Port Vieux
Restaurant (features *niçoise* specialities), shows and dancing.
Smart Club, 25 Promenade des Anglais
Disco; opens at 10.30pm.

St Tropez
Les Caves du Roy, Hotel Byblos.
Tel: 94 97 00 04.
Legendary banquets; reserve 1–2 days ahead.
L'Eequinade, Near the city hall.
Disco, opens at 11pm, admission 80FF.
Le Papagayo, Residence du Port.
Disco, opens at 11pm, admission 80FF.

Golf

Biot
Bastide du Roy.
Tel: 93 65 08 48.

Cannes
Mandelieu la Napoule.
Tel: 93 49 55 39.

La Londe les Maures
Domaine de Valcros.
Tel: 94 66 81 02.

Monaco
La Turbie.
Tel: 93 41 09 11.

Eze Country Club. Accessible via the D45. Tel: 93 41 24 64

Mougins
175 Route d'Antibes.
Tel: 93 75 79 13.

Nice
698 Route de Grenoble.
Tel: 93 29 82 00.

Roquebrune/Argens
Domaine des Planes.
Tel: 94 82 92 91.

St Maxime
Boulevard des Collines.
Tel: 94 96 16 98.

St Raphael
Quartier de Valescure.
Tel: 94 52 16 58

Valbonne
Route de Roquefort.
Tel: 93 42 00 00.

Riding

Colle S Loup
Route de Montegros.
Tel: 93 32 68 33.

Eze
Crazy Horse Club, Plateau de la Justice, 8 Grand Corniche.
Tel: 93 01 84 11.
Cercle Hippique du Col d'Eze
Tel: 93 41 25 95.

Grasse
Route de Grasse.
Tel: 93 09 12 32.
270 Route de Cannes.
Tel: 93 70 55 41.

Mandelieu
Club San Estello (RN17).
Tel: 93 93 14 18.

Mougins
909 Chemin Font de Curaner.
Tel: 93 45 75 81.
Nice
368 Route de Grenoble.
Tel: 93 13 13 16.

Roquefort
Chemin Taures.
Tel: 93 77 51 64.

St Paul
600 Chemin Malvan.
Tel: 93 32 96 84.

St Tropez
Domaine de Beauvallon.
Tel: 94 56 16 55.

Vence
Col de Vence.
Tel: 93 24 65 00.

Villeneuve-Loubet
Route de Grasse.
Tel: 93 20 99 64.

Hiking Paths
Le Santier des Balcons de la Côte d'Azur leads from Menton into the Esterel through more than 100 miles (160km) of countryside (GR51). Hiking guides with routes (*Sentiers Tour istique*) and maps are available in newsagents and bookshops.

Boat Rental

Antibes
Poxile Marine. Tel: 93 34 60 41.
Eric Sport. Tel: 93 34 67 51.
L'Ile Bleue. Tel: 93 34 64 65.

Cannes
Camper et Nicholsons.
Tel: 93 43 16 75.
Navimer Intern. Tel: 93 47 21 85.
Map Home. Tel: 93 90 28 98.
Marcelle Senesi. Tel: 93 99 03 51.

Juan les Pins
Sam Boat Location.
Tel: 93 61 23 04.
Aquasport. Tel: 93
61 20 01.
Mandelieu:
Challenge des
mers. Tel: 93 93
12 34.

Monaco:
Camper et Nicholson.
Tel: 93 50 84 86.

Speed Limits
Max speed 5 knots 1,000ft (300m)
from the coast; in busy waters (for example near the Lêrins Islands and before Villefranche) the maximum is 12
knots.

MARKETS

Antibes
Cours Masséna. Daily except Monday,
from 6am–noon.
Flea market. Thursday on Place Au-
diberti.
Handicrafts. Cours Masséna: Tuesday,
Friday and Saturday starting at 2pm.
Clothing. Place A Barnaud: Thursday
and Saturday mornings.

Cagnes-sur-Mer
Centre Ville. Pedestrian zone, daily
except Monday.

Cannes
Flower Market. Rue Félix Faure, daily
except Monday.
Flea market. Rue Félix Faure, Saturday.
Marché Fortville. Rue Maynadier:
daily except Monday.

Grasse
Place aux Aires. Daily except Monday.

Fréjus
Place de Piovriers. Wednesday and
Sat-
urday mornings.
Flower Market. Place de
la Mairie: Wednesday and Saturday
mornings.

Menton
Halles. Daily, not Monday.
Flea market. Place aux Herbes, Friday.
Clothing market. Halles, Saturday.

Monaco
**Marché Condamine/Marché Monte
Carlo**. Every morning, except Monday.

Nice
**Marché Saleya/Marché Libera-
tion/Marché Fontaine du Temple**.
Every morning except Monday.
Flea market. Cour Saleya, Monday.
Fish market. Place St Francois, every
morning except Monday.

Vence
Little Market. Place Clemenceau, Tuesday mornings.
Large Market. Place Clemenceau, Friday mornings.

Index

ART / PHOTO CREDITS

Cover Design   **Klaus Geisler**
Cartography   **Berndtson & Berndtson**

NOTES

Senez

Barrage de Castillon

Ubraye

Chiran 1905

Blieux

Demandolx

Brianconnet

Sallagriffon

Castellane

Barrage de Chaudanne

St.Auban

Estéron

Gironde

Estéro

MONTAGNE

Cir Ch

Verdon

Peyroules

Thorenc

1

Torrent de Valonge

Point Sublime

Rougon

Le Mousteiret

Gréolières

Loup

GRAND CANYON DU VERDON

Le Bourguet

Brenon

Séranon

MONTAGNE DE L'AUDIBERGUE

Caussols

GRAND PLAN DE CANJUERS

La Gournuelle

La Bastide

Escragnolles

St.Vallier- de- Thiey

Comps-S.-Artuby

La Roque-Esclapon

Mons

Grass

MONTAGNE DE BARJAUDE

Vérignon

Bargemon

FRANCE

Fayence

Cabris

Le Tignet

Montauroux

Aups

Montferrat

Callas

Tanneron

Pég

Ampus

Reboullon

St.Paul-en- Forêt

Lac de St.Cassien

MASSIF DU TANNERON

Salernes

Draguignan

St.Pons

Enore

Bagnois-en- Forêt

Reyran

Les Adrets de-l'Esterel

Mandelieu

Maure-Viell

Bresque

Flayosc

La Motte

Catchéou

Le Capitou

Mont Vinaigre 618

M

Entecasteaux

Lorgues

Le Muy

Puget-sur-Argens

MASSIF DE L'ESTEREL

Agay

Argens

Les Arcs

Tarandeau

Vidauban

Argens

Roquebrune-sur-Argens

Fréjus

Valescure

Le Dramont

Anthéor

Le Thoronet

Aille

St.Raphaël

Cap du Dramont

Golfe de Frejus

St.Aygulf

Le Luc

Le Cannet des- Maures

MAURES

Plan- de-la-Tour

San- Peire-sur- Mer

Les Issambres

CORNICHE

Flassans-sur- Issole

Aille

La Nartelle

Pignans

Gonfaron

Les Mayons

La Garde- Freinet

Préconil

Beauvallon

St.Maxime

Réal Martin

Valescure

DES

Golfe

de St.Tropez

Cap de St.Tropez

Collobrières

Cogolin

St.Tropez

MASSIF

La Verne

La Môle

Môle

La Croix Valmer

Gassin

Plage de Tahiti

Plage de Pampelonne

Les Pradels 528

Cap Caramat

Pas- du- Cert

Môle

Cavalaire-sur- Mer

Plage de Escalet

Réserve du Trapan

Bormes-les- Mimosas

Cavalière

Cap Ladier

CORNICHE DES MAURES

Cap Cartaya

Plage de la Briande

ITALY

San Remo

Sospel
Airole
Col de Braus
Bévera
Dolceacqua
Castillon
Pic de Baudon
▲ 1264

L'Escarène
Contes
Gorbio
Ventimiglia
Bordighera
Castagniers
Mortola
Cantaron
Menton
RIVIERA DI PONENTE
Cap- Martin
Beausoleil
Gattières
Monte- Carlo
MONACO
Bonson
Gilette
Levens
Vence
La Barenne
Nice
Beaulieu- sur- Mer
Villefranche
St.Jean- Cap- Ferrat
St.Laurent- du- Var
Plage de la Ville
Cap Ferrat
Cagnes
Biot
Villeneuve- Loubet- Plage
Airport Nice- Côte d'Azur
Zoo marin
Vallauris
Antibes
Golfe- Juan
net
Juan- les- Pins
Golfe Juan
Cap d'Antibes
Ile St.Marguerite
Ile St.Honorat
ES DE LÉRINS

RON
Var
segoules
oup

Ferry to Bastia

C O T E   D ' A Z U R

Ferry to Ajaccio, Propriano, Calvi, Ile Rousse

Mediterranean

Sea

Côte d'Azur

16 km / 10 miles